Getting the Signals Right: Tax Reform to Protect the Environment and the Economy

DAVID MALIN ROODMAN

Jane A. Peterson, *Editor*

WORLDWATCH PAPER 134
May 1997

FINANCIAL SUPPORT is provided by the Nathan Cummings Foundation, the Geraldine R. Dodge Foundation, The Ford Foundation, The William and Flora Hewlett Foundation, W. Alton Jones Foundation, John D. and Catherine T. MacArthur Foundation, Charles Stewart Mott Foundation, The Curtis and Edith Munson Foundation, The Pew Charitable Trusts, Rasmussen Foundation, Rockefeller Brothers Fund, Rockefeller Financial Services, Turner Foundation, U.N. Population Fund, Wallace Genetic Foundation, Wallace Global Fund, Weeden Foundation, the Winslow Foundation, and a personal contribution from Robert Wallace.

Table of Contents

Tables and Figures

The views expressed are those of the author(s) and do not necessarily represent those of the Worldwatch Institute, its directors, officers, or staff, or of its funding organizations.

Acknowledgments: I thank Nils Axel Braathen, Clifford Cobb, and Stefan Speck, along with Worldwatch colleagues Lester R. Brown, Christopher Flavin, Hilary French, Gary Gardner, William H. Mansfield III, Anne Platt McGinn, and Michael Renner, for reviewing earlier drafts of this paper. I thank also the many people who have given of their time over the last two years to help me explore the wide and complex terrain of the tax issue. Thanks too to Lori Ann Baldwin and Laura Malinowski for responding quickly to requests for books and articles; to Jim Perry, Denise Byers Thomma, and Mary Caron for spirited efforts to carry this paper's message to the press; and to editor Jane Peterson for patience and humor throughout a difficult process.

David Malin Roodman is a Senior Researcher at the Worldwatch Institute, where he investigates the economics and political economy of environmental problems. He has also written about energy policy and the human and ecological impacts of buildings. He contributes regularly to the Institute's annuals, *State of the World* and *Vital Signs*, and to its magazine, *World Watch*. He authored Worldwatch Paper 133, *Paying the Piper: Subsidies, Politics, and the Environment*, released in December 1996. Mr. Roodman graduated from Harvard College with a Bachelor's degree in pure mathematics. He then spent a year at the University of Cambridge, U.K., where his interests shifted to the relationships between economy and environment.

Introduction

M ost people sense that something is not right with our relationship with the earth. Perhaps some wipe thick dust from their city windowsills, wondering if it is laced with lead. Others may worry that the chemicals they spray on crops are leaching into the groundwater their children drink. Or maybe in a warm winter's week, they recall reports that rising seas, retreating glaciers, and freakish weather are persuading most climatologists that global warming has arrived.[1]

Yet despite widespread awareness of environmental problems, many people fear that solving them will cost too much. Doesn't solar energy cost more than coal? Don't regulations hurt industry and eliminate jobs? Societies are paralyzed by a paradox: seemingly, we cannot afford to protect the environment—but neither can we afford not to.

What creates this paradox is that most activities in industrial countries today come with two price tags, one visible, one hidden. In Germany, for example, making electricity from coal costs a utility 6 cents per kilowatt-hour—but it costs the population at large an additional 2 cents, considering the disease and death caused by air pollution. If utilities had to pay those costs too, windpower would suddenly become much more competitive—and profitable. But they need not, so coal remains king. Indeed, almost every artifact of the global industrial economy carries some environmental cost that is hidden and thus easily ignored.[2]

To end the paralysis that blocks environmental progress, governments need to close the gap between real and false prices. The most direct way to do that is to impose taxes—

taxes on pollution, resource depletion, and ecosystem degradation. Equivalently, governments can auction off permits for those activities, then allow businesses to trade the permits among themselves. Either way, putting a price on pollution enforces an idea at once radical and commonsensical: that people should pay the full costs of the harm they do others. Once this principle is enforced, environmental protection becomes not just a cost, but a profit opportunity. And unlike most regulations, which set minimum standards, tax incentives create an ongoing prod for improvement without restricting people's flexibility in responding. Experiences in the United States, the Netherlands, and Singapore show that businesses leap on such opportunities, creating technologies that conserve resources and slash pollution rates, often at surprisingly low cost. Environmental taxes thus exploit humanity's greatest resource: its creativity in problem solving.

This market-harnessing ability of tax and permit systems makes them perhaps the most powerful tools available for ending the global economy's tendency to undermine its own ecological foundations and damage human health. They can, for example, curtail urban air and water pollution; slow fishing and groundwater overpumping; knit today's mine-to-landfill material flows into recycling loops; and smooth the transition from fossil fuels to solar and wind power. Indeed, many countries have begun to apply tax and permit systems to such problems. In the face of these urgent challenges, such effective tools are essentially indispensable.

Not only can tax and permit systems guide economic development in a direction that makes sense in the long run: they can do so without hurting economies today by shifting the tax burden rather than increasing it. Environmental taxes or permit sales can raise trillions of dollars that can go toward cutting taxes that penalize work and investment. Fully 90 percent of the $7.5 trillion in tax revenues raised each year worldwide come from levies on payrolls, personal income, corporate profits, capital gains, retail sales, trade, and built property. A carbon tax on coal, oil, and natural gas alone could raise roughly a trillion dollars per year worldwide. That revenue could pay for a 20 percent cut in conventional taxes—on wages, for example. The new tax would force some fossil-fuel-intensive businesses to retrench and cut payrolls, but other firms would expand thanks to the labor tax cut, generating even more jobs. Meanwhile, carbon dioxide emissions would fall, reducing the risks global warming poses for agriculture and coastal cities. (Governments can cut conventional taxes even more if they reduce *subsidies* for environmentally destructive activities, as the previous Worldwatch Paper argued.)[3]

Environmental tax and permit systems can also make the transition to an environmentally sound economy gradual and predictable. A carbon tax, for example, could start low and then rise over 20 years, allowing many of today's cars and factories to live out their useful lives. Preannouncing tax increases would send a powerful signal on an economy's future direction while allowing businesses to plan ahead.[4]

Tax reform is already a perennial topic of debate in many countries. In the United States, there have recently been calls for a flat tax and for a much lower capital gains tax—essentially different ways to tax work and investment. Most of their proponents have hardly paused to examine the bigger picture, to ask whether governments should so heavily penalize what they want to encourage, and barely tax what they want to discourage. The levies that now dominate tax codes all have their virtues, including the ability to spread the cost of government according to people's ability to pay. But they are also creatures of an era when people could ignore their economic dependence on the environment.

The recognition that tax codes have fallen dangerously behind the times has begun to dawn on many policymakers. One reason the environmental tax idea has caught on but slowly despite a 75-year pedigree in the economic literature is that environmentalists have historically preferred the surety of regulation over the more hands-off tax approach. But many now perceive the virtue of harnessing industry's problem-solving ability. And they are not alone. Polls in the European Union and the United States have found that 70 percent of respondents support the idea of "green tax reform," once it is explained. Many political parties in Northern Europe have endorsed it, as have the European Trade Union Confederation and the Union of Industrial and Employers' Confederation of Europe. But outside of Europe, the idea by and large has yet to reach either policymakers or the public.[5]

Nonetheless, countries ranging from Canada to China levy thousands of environmental taxes altogether, on everything from gasoline and pesticides to sulfur and carbon emissions—though only a few dozen standouts have been implemented in ways that do much environmental good. The Netherlands has used levies to dramatically reduce water pollution. The United States has used them to phase out ozone-depleting chemicals. New Zealand regulates most of its fisheries with tradable permit systems. And since 1991, five European countries have taken the seminal step of combining environmental tax hikes with income or payroll tax cuts.[6]

Tax and permit systems are promising medicine, but applied on their own, they are neither cure-alls nor side-effect-free. Thus, drivers will not respond well to the stick of a gasoline tax, for example, unless offered the carrot of zoning laws and mass transit budgets that support independence from the auto. Similarly, pensioners struggling to keep up with rising heating oil prices will take little solace in sacrificing for society as a whole. So tax and permit systems should not be applied puritanically. Rather, like changes to a city's street plan, they are best implemented gradually, with prior notice, and with assistance for those least able to adapt.

Choosing which taxes to cut also requires sensitivity to local circumstance. In developing countries, tax cuts for investment, labor, or sales could reduce one obstacle to economic growth. In the Western industrial world, cuts could be aimed at what political leaders there often call the most worrisome economic ailment, the erosion of the middle class. Payroll tax cuts could increase after-tax paychecks and, in the long run, the incentive for people to invest in the training and education that lead to better jobs; they could also make employees cheaper for employers, boosting job growth. Of course as environmental damage decreased, revenues from environmental taxes would drop, and the tax shift would have to partly reverse. But in the case of the biggest taxes, like those on carbon emissions, the decline might not start for decades, resulting in change that is moderately paced by the standards of tax history.[7]

Overall, countries have barely scratched the surface of the potential of tax shifting. The global economy has hardly been perturbed from its ecologically insupportable course. Delving deeper will not be easy. Businesses on the losing side of any tax shift are often the best financed and organized. Fortunately, environmental tax shifting creates more winners than losers, since every cut in one person's taxes is a rise in someone else's, and everyone would gain from a healthier environment. The task for environmental tax reformers is to build alliances with the winning majority. They can find common ground with labor unions that favor wage tax cuts, with minimally polluting service businesses that would receive more from reductions in conventional taxes than they would pay in environmental taxes, and with vendors of environmentally protective goods and services—participants in a market projected to be worth $572 billion already by the year 2001. Given the formidable resistance to environmental tax shifting, the challenge of securing the earth is ultimately one of educating and persuading the public.[8]

"Making the Polluter Pay"

Environmental taxes are perhaps the most powerful tool societies have for forging economies that protect human and environmental health. For people accustomed to thinking of taxes as a necessary evil, it may come as a surprise that some taxes can do economies good. Yet taxing environmentally harmful activities—or, to the same effect, auctioning limited numbers of permits for engaging in them—discourages activities that do more harm than good to society as a whole. This is actually a case where it is better to tax than not to tax.

Famed British economist Arthur C. Pigou was the first to advocate environmental taxes. In his 1920 classic, *The Economics of Welfare*, he pointed to the hidden costs of the sulfur and smoke pouring from coal-burning factories and fireplaces in Manchester, England. Costs of extra laundry cleaning, of artificial lighting necessitated by darkened air, and of repairs to corroded buildings had been estimated at £290,000 per year (about $10 million a year at today's prices). As a result, a steelmaker might have made £100 worth of steel from a furnaceful of coal, and done £200 in damage in the process—a gain for the company, but a net loss for the city. In effect, pollution victims were subsidizing pollution causers, and making society as a whole poorer.[9]

The problem, as recently put by Ernst von Weizsäcker, president of the Wuppertal Institute in Germany and a leading environmental tax advocate, is that prices do not "tell the ecological truth." The solution, Pigou argued, is for governments to use taxes to make degraders of the environment pay the economic costs of the harm they do. Then when they tallied up the costs and benefits of environmental harm for themselves, they would have to take society's interests into account.[10]

In the Netherlands, a set of charges originally intended only to cover the costs of wastewater treatment has produced a classic demonstration of the pollution-preventing power of charges themselves. Since 1970, gradually rising

FIGURE 1

Industrial Discharges of Selected Heavy Metals into Surface Waters, the Netherlands, 1976–94

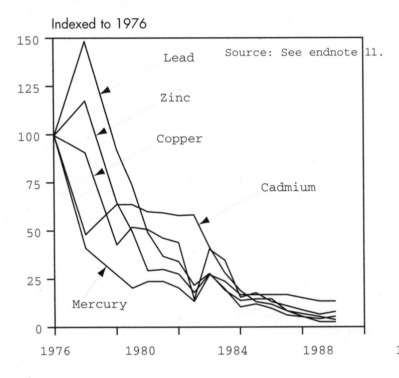

fees for emissions of organic material and heavy metals into canals, rivers, and lakes have spurred companies to cut emissions, but without dictating how. Between 1976 and 1994, emissions of cadmium, copper, lead, mercury, and zinc plummeted 86–97 percent, primarily because of the charges, according to statistical analyses. (See Figure 1.) Companies for whom cleaning up was cheapest probably did it most. Firms may also have passed part of the taxes on to their customers through higher prices, causing them to switch to less-pollution-intensive products. And demand for pollution control equipment has spurred Dutch manufacturers to develop better models, lowering costs and turning the country into a global leader in the market. The taxes have in effect sought the path of least economic resistance—of least cost—in cleaning up the country's waters.[11]

Instead of taxing pollution or resource depletion, governments can auction off limited numbers of permits for the right to do the same thing. A company that then decides to pollute or deplete more than it is entitled to has to buy extra permits from ones that agree to do so less. To phase out the use of ozone-depleting chlorofluorocarbons (CFCs), for instance, Singapore has been distributing declining numbers of permits on a quarterly basis for producing or importing the chemicals. It gives half to companies for free, based on past CFC use, and auctions the rest to the highest bidders. It does essentially the same for new cars, to control the crowded city-state's automobile fleet. (In 1992, the cost of a permit represented about a quarter of the price of a new Honda Civic.)[12]

Through such tradable permit systems, societies can cap the amount of pollution or resource use that will take place each year, and then allow the market to settle on a price for it. Taxes, by contrast, set the price and let the market decide the amount. These policies are more alike than different: both can raise revenue, and both exploit the market to protect the environment. (Because of their kinship, the approaches will often be referred to collectively as "environmental taxes.")

In 1992, the U.S. Environmental Protection Agency (EPA) created the world's largest environmental permit trading system, designed to control emissions of sulfur dioxide (SO_2), an acid rain ingredient. The EPA is allocating enough permits to utilities and other polluters so that emissions in 2000 will occur at only half the 1980 rate. Fewer permit trades have occurred than most observers had hoped, but enough to put a price on sulfur emissions. During the legislative battle over the bill, industry had predicted the price would settle at $1,650 per ton; the EPA put the figure around $660, and environmental groups estimated $330. All were wrong. Today a one-ton permit costs about $70.[13]

Cutting emissions, in other words, has proved far cheaper than almost anyone expected, so companies have been unwilling to spend much in the permit market in order to emit extra. Even companies that do not trade have more flexibility in meeting emissions requirements. For example, they can install sulfur-collecting "scrubbers," switch to low-sulfur coal, or opt for natural gas. "You don't need a large volume of trades to have an impact," reports James Potts, a vice-president of the Potomac Electric Power Company in Washington, D.C. "When we went out for competitive bids for lower sulfur coal... those bids came in very, very competitive." Sulfur scrubber prices have tumbled too. As a result, industry will save an estimated $1.9–3.1 billion a year by 2002 compared with what the traditional regulatory approach would have cost.[14]

The U.S. trading system, like most to date, deviates from the ideal in one important respect. Rather than auctioning off the permits, worth millions of dollars altogether, it takes the politically easier course of giving them away. In doing so, it subsidizes established firms for past emissions even as it taxes them for current ones. That handicaps newcomers not grandfathered into the system, and slows the economy by forgoing a chance to cut taxes on work and investment.[15]

The experiences in the Netherlands, Singapore, and the United States nevertheless demonstrate how market-based policies can help societies meet environmental goals. The conceptually tougher challenge is to *set* those goals—to determine what tax rate to use or how many permits to allocate. Economists usually argue that governments should allow environmental harm just up to the point where the costs for society begin to outweigh the economic benefits. But environmental problems, like most important policy issues, involve more than costs and benefits: they also involve rights and wrongs, values and vision. (If crime paid, cost-benefit analysis would endorse it.) In Pigou's time, between 1873 and 1892, London smogs are thought to have taken at least 2,000 lives. Today, air pollution affects 1.1 billion city dwellers worldwide, prematurely ending 300,000–700,000 lives a year and causing chronic coughing in at least 50 million children. Since the value of human life and health is not fully expressible in dollar terms, there can be no one right price for pollution.[16]

Likewise, resource depletion can carry a hidden, but hard-to-quantify, cost: that of depriving future generations of limited and essentially irreplaceable natural resources. As pioneering environmental economist Herman Daly has pointed out, today's financial markets force human-made and natural capital to compete on equal footing, even though one is easily replaceable and one not. Fish and forests that cannot grow as fast as investments in corporations, the market says, should be liquidated, consumed as if there were no tomorrow. As a result, we seem to be bequeathing to generations a century hence as much financial wealth as we can—and a world empty of fish and old-growth forests. That prospect gives cause for government intervention. But what moral weight to give future generations' needs for topsoil or natural gas is ultimately an ethical decision, not just an economic one.[17]

However sacred these values, completely protecting them may be impractical in the short run. If suddenly taken literally, the right to breathe air that does not shorten one's life, for instance, would spell chaos for millions of car- or moped-dependent workers and their families. This conflict is nothing new: whenever policymakers regulate or tax, or even decide to do nothing, they make impossible tradeoffs between jobs and health, profits and nature. Societies need to resolve these conflicts over time; for example, they may develop vehicles running on solar electricity, or accept some pollution, such as noise on city streets, as a practical necessity. What matters is that they strive to make the tradeoffs pragmatically, yet in accordance with collective values.[18]

For market-based environmental policies, that means not worrying over the exact tax rate or permit allocation. Instead policymakers can start taxes low, and permit allocations generous, and tighten the constraints over time, in order to send a powerful but minimally disruptive signal that economies must move toward configurations that protect the earth and respect people's rights to a healthy environment.

How fast taxes should rise will depend on the seriousness of the environmental problem at hand and the difficulty of solving it. In the United States, for example, the tax on CFCs started at $3.02 per kilogram in 1990 and climbed to $11.80 by the time the chemicals were completely phased out six years later. Both the immediacy of the ozone problem and ready availability of CFC substitutes sped the transition. In contrast, curtailing fossil fuel dependence in order to halt global warming will take decades, so a more gradual rise in the price of carbon emissions may be appropriate. That would give carmakers, for example, lead time and incentive to develop vehicles powered by solar electricity, and make it more profitable for developers to build neighborhoods where people can walk more than drive. Governments would also have time to help coal miners find new jobs and low-income people insulate their homes.[19]

Policymakers can start taxes low and raise them over time, to send a powerful, minimally disruptive signal.

The appropriate tempo for other environmental problems would lie between these two extremes. In arid regions, taxes on groundwater overdrafting might lead over several decades to widespread adoption of Israeli-developed drip irrigation technologies that cut water use 70 percent. Rising duties on air and water pollution would encourage chemical companies to gradually reformulate their production processes to generate fewer toxic byproducts—or to capture them for use in other processes. In the same fashion, levies on mining, unsustainable logging, landfilling, and waste incineration could launch a transformation of today's throwaway economy into a reusing, recycling economy. Instead of mining mountains of virgin ore, companies would mine the mountains of solid waste accumulating outside towns and cities. Whatever the time frame, the sooner tax and permit phase-ins begin, the more gradual and less disruptive they can be.[20]

Environmental Taxes, Today and Tomorrow

From water pollution charges in the Netherlands to air pollution levies in China, thousands of environmental taxes, as well as a few permit systems, are now in use, many adopted within the last 15 years. These initial forays into environmental protection through taxation have often been cautious or ineffective, and even the best examples fall far short of preserving the environment on which the global economy depends. But some have clearly demonstrated the potential of market-based approaches. And policymakers are at least learning from each other's failures and successes, engaging in a process as old as civilization: adapting the tax code to the times. (See Table 1.) It remains to be seen whether they will carry the new approach out of this early, experimental phase, and into the mainstreams of fiscal and environmental policy. What is clear is that it has much more to offer.[21]

Surprisingly, some of the least market-reliant countries levy what are, on paper, the world's most sophisticated environmental taxes. In China, Poland, Russia, and other traditionally communist countries, tax regimes now apply to hundreds of air and water pollutants, toxic and radioactive waste, and even noise. The systems have developed over the last 20 years out of a communist tradition of using fines to enforce environmental standards, and in response to the particularly ruinous environmental toll of central planning. They are used mostly for funding environmental protection agencies, as well as for grants and subsidized loans to industry for pollution control investment. In Poland, revenues are relatively high at 1 percent of total tax receipts.[22]

These pollution levy systems are, however, generally more impressive in theory than in practice. Emissions below officially permitted levels are usually exempted from taxation. And corruption and inflation in the 1990s have wiped out much of the taxes' incentive effect. In addition, many companies are still state-run monopolies and can pass their costs on to the government or customers, making them unresponsive to market signals. Nevertheless, the charge systems are a foundation for what could eventually become a set of robust environmental taxes. The government of China seems particularly keen to press forward. By 2001, it plans to extend existing taxes to emissions *within* permitted levels, and establish new ones to attack acid rain and water pollution.[23]

Other developing countries use environmental taxes with more effect, if less sophistication. Malaysia has adjusted its gas taxes to make leaded fuel 2.8 percent more expensive than unleaded. Partly as a result, unleaded gasoline has grabbed more than 60 percent of the market. Since lead has been linked to brain damage in children, there seems little doubt that the modest charge has easily paid for itself. Thailand and Turkey also favor unleaded fuel with lower taxes. Costa Rica lays a 15 percent duty on oil products in order to pass some of the costs of road construction back to drivers. A third of the proceeds go to pay small farmers to plant trees, which soak up heat-trapping carbon dioxide as they grow, partly compensating for emissions from driving.[24]

Some developing countries also use tradable permits. Chile has auctioned permits to regulate fishing for some species as well as agricultural water use. Farmers in parts of Algeria, Brazil, India, Mexico, Morocco, Pakistan, Peru, and Tunisia trade water rights. Many of these systems developed without formal government involvement and are quite old. In the southern part of the Brazilian state of Ceará, farmers have traded water rights for at least a century.[25]

Western industrial countries have made the greatest use of environmental tax and permit systems. One group of well-established taxes—those on energy sources—raised more than $243 billion in 1993, or 3.8 percent of total tax

TABLE 1

Selected Experiences with Environmental Tax and Permit Systems

Policy, Country, First Year in Effect	Description
Overfishing Fishing permit systems, New Zealand, 1986	Overfishing reduced. Many stocks appear to be rebuilding. Fishing industry, unlike that of most countries, seems stable and profitable despite lack of subsidies.
Excessive Water Demand Tradable water rights, Chile, 1981	Existing users grandfathered. Rights to new supplies auctioned. Total water use capped.
Solid Waste Toxic waste charge, Germany, 1991	Toxic waste production fell more than 15 percent in 3 years.
Solid waste charge, Denmark, 1986	Recycling rate for demolition waste shot from 12 to 82 percent over 6–8 years.
Water Pollution Fees to cover waste-water treatment costs, Netherlands, 1970	Main factor behind 86–97 percent drop in industrial heavy metals discharges and substantial drops in organic emissions.
Fertilizer sales taxes, Sweden, 1982 and 1984	One charge, 1982–92, funded agricultural subsidies; the other pays for education programs on fertilizer use reduction. Use of nitrogen dropped 25 percent; potassium, 60 percent; phosphorus, 64 percent.
Acid Rain Nitrogen oxide charge on electricity producers, Sweden, 1992	Refunded as electricity production subsidy. Contributed to 35 percent emissions reduction in two years.
Sulfur permit system, United States, 1995	Nearly all permits allocated free to past emitters. Forcing total emissions to about half the 1980 level by 2000; cost of compliance far lower than predicted.

Global Atmospheric Disruption

Ozone-depleting substance tax, United States, 1990	Smoothing and enforcing phase-outs.
Chlorofluorocarbon permit system, Singapore, 1989	Half of permits auctioned, half allocated to past producers and importers. Smoothing and enforcing phase-out.
Carbon dioxide tax, Norway, 1991	Emissions appear 3–4 percent lower than they would have been without the tax.

Uncontrolled Development

Tradable development rights, New Jersey Pinelands, 1982	Land use plan sets density limits on development in forested, agricultural, and designated growth zones. In growth zones, developers may build beyond density limits if they buy credits from landowners agreeing to develop less than they could. Owners of 5,870 hectares in more-protected areas have sold off development rights.

General

Linking of investment tax credits to environmental and employment records, Louisiana, 1991	Tax credits reduced up to 50 percent for firms that pollute most and employ least. Twelve firms agreed to cut toxic emissions enough to lower the state's total by 8.2 percent. Repealed after one year.

Source: See endnote 21.

revenues, mostly from duties on gasoline and diesel fuel (figures also include taxes on the carbon-dioxide-generating potential of fossil fuels). Duties on motor vehicle ownership brought in another $39 billion, or 0.6 percent of revenues. The United States has by far the lowest gasoline taxes, averaging 9 cents per liter (34 cents per gallon) in 1994, while taxes in Australia, Canada, Japan, and New Zealand lie in the range of 20–30 cents per liter ($0.75–1.14 per gallon). In

Europe, taxes of 40–85 cents per liter ($1.51–3.22 per gallon) push pump prices two to four times higher than in the United States. Gas taxes are especially high in Southern Europe, accounting for 5–10 percent of tax revenues. Many factors, including population density, city planning, and convenience of public transit, shape people's decisions about what size cars to buy and how much to drive them. But the influence of gas price is obvious to any visitor to the United States or Italy: where gas is cheap, minivans and sport-utility vehicles roam the roads in droves; where it is pricey, petite autos vie with mopeds for pavement. (See Figure 2.)[26]

In addition, hundreds of less conventional environmental tax, permit, and deposit-refund systems are now operating in western industrial countries, applying to everything from beverage containers in Belgium to car batteries in Canada. Altogether they raise some $63 billion per year, or 1.0 percent of total revenue. In a few countries, they raise more. Denmark got 4.0 percent of its revenue from environmental taxes in 1993, and the Netherlands, 5.1 percent (excluding carbon taxes).[27]

Some of these taxes are levied by local authorities to solve local problems. Others are applied by national governments in the face of global ones. The United States, Denmark, and Australia have combined regulations and taxes to phase out production of ozone-depleting chemicals, including CFCs by 1996. Between 1990 and 1996, the U.S. tax raised $4.1 billion, and appeared to have accelerated the phase-out beyond what the regulations required. In its first year, an SO_2 tax in Sweden apparently reduced emissions 5 percent, and another tax led to a 35 percent drop in emissions of nitrogen oxides (NO_x, also an acid-rain ingredient) in its first year, according to Sweden's Ministry of the Environment and Natural Resources. After Denmark instituted a solid waste charge, the share of demolition refuse that went unrecycled crumpled from 88 to 18 percent. Denmark is also one of the few countries to directly tax the depletion of a natural resource, specifically, sand and gravel, the most valuable grades of which are being rapidly consumed for road and building construction.[28]

FIGURE 2

Gasoline Price versus Use, Western Industrial Countries, 1994

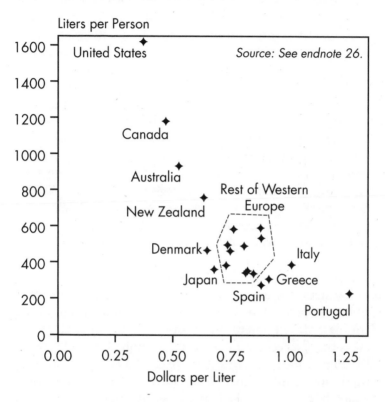

In what may eventually be seen as the most important environmental tax development of the 1990s, five countries—Denmark, Finland, the Netherlands, Norway, and Sweden—have introduced duties on emissions of heat-trapping carbon dioxide from burning coal, oil, and natural gas. In practice though, the most carbon-intensive industries like steelmaking are at least partially exempt from these taxes, which blunts their effect.[29]

While Europe has used taxes the most, other industrial countries have developed more experience with tradable permits. Copying the federal sulfur trading system, authorities in Massachusetts and Southern California are instituting permit schemes to reduce local air pollution from factories and power plants. Tradable permits now govern almost all of New Zealand's fisheries, and a few in Australia, the United States, and Canada. Villagers in Alicante, in Spain's arid southern half, can be forgiven if these developments leave them unimpressed; they and their ancestors have traded water rights since the mid-1200s.[30]

Some of the most innovative environmental tax and permit systems to date have been developed by U.S. state governments. Arid Arizona instituted perhaps the world's only groundwater depletion tax, in the Phoenix region in 1991. On the opposite side of the continent, New Jersey has used permits to add flexibility to its plan to protect the Pinelands, a 445,000-hectare region of wildlife habitat, berry farms, and small towns under strong development pressure. After extensive consultations with residents, the state set limits on building density in designated forest, farm, and town zones. Since the state believed that the character of the region was threatened by both the amount of construction and its dispersion across the landscape, it then established a trading system to facilitate more-compact development. Developers in designated growth areas can exceed local construction limits if they buy credits from landowners in other areas who agree to build less than they could. Since 1982, owners in more-protected zones have traded away in perpetuity rights to build on 5,870 hectares.[31]

Another creative market mechanism appeared in the heavily polluted state of Louisiana in 1991. The government there began grading companies on compliance with environmental laws and the number of people they employed for the amount of pollution they generated. Companies with low scores lost up to half the standard tax deduction for new investment. In the first year, 12 firms agreed to cut toxic emissions enough to lower the state's total by 8.2 percent. Many of the pollution reduction plans cost the companies more than they earned in tax credits, showing that the fear of a tarnished public image was giving the tax system added kick. Businesses disliked it so much that they fought successfully for its repeal in 1992.[32]

More than they may realize, today's environmental tax experimenters are following in the footsteps of their predecessors, for the early history of today's most important taxes was similarly halting. Austria, the Netherlands, and Great Britain, for example, made early use of the income tax to fund the wars against Napoleon. In Britain, the House of Commons reintroduced the tax in the 1840s and cut import duties on grain, butter, and cheese in order to quell unrest among urban poor verging on starvation. It was again a supposedly temporary measure, but food riots and rising demands on the treasury made this nineteenth-century tax shift permanent. In the United States, the income tax was first pressed into service during the Civil War, later struck down by the Supreme Court, and finally backed by constitutional amendment in 1913. Since World War II, broad-based taxes on sales, profits, wages, and income have ballooned to account for the majority of government receipts in industrial countries.[33]

If environmental taxes follow a similar trajectory, the mainstays of today's tax codes probably will not disappear, but they will decline in importance. Environmental taxes, if they seriously confront the challenge of achieving sustainability, could bring in far more revenue than they do today. One way to see this is by leafing through the proliferating studies of the economic costs of environmental harm. The hidden costs of driving in the United States, for example, include lung disease, global warming, injuries and deaths from accidents, wasted time in traffic jams, and property value drops near busy roads. They total roughly $218 billion per year (1995 dollars), according to a 1994 study by Charles Komanoff, a New York-based analyst. That hidden cost equals some $830 per person, 3 percent of gross domestic product (GDP). Passing it back to drivers would take a tax of 41 cents per liter of motor fuel ($1.56 per gallon) and could supplant 11 percent of current tax revenue. It would double what Americans pay at the pump—to about the price of

milk. (But if channeled into cutting the employee-paid payroll tax, it could give most workers a 6 percent raise.) Similar
studies have concluded that even in Western Europe fuel
taxes would need to rise to pass the full costs of driving back
to drivers.[34]

Some studies have measured the economic costs of a
suite of environmental problems at once. To arrive at their
bottom lines, they count everything from the cost of replac-
ing the water purification services of destroyed wetlands to
that of building dikes against a rising sea. Various studies
have tallied environmental costs at 2 percent of GDP in
Australia and Japan, 12–15 percent in China, 23 percent in
Germany, 40 percent in Sweden, and 45 percent in the
United States. The spread is wide because different studies
count different damages or the same damages in different
ways. Most importantly, global warming and fossil fuel
depletion, which account for 60–70 percent of the costs
reported for Germany, Sweden, and the United States, are
not considered in the other studies.[35]

Since environmental tax and permit auctions work by
raising revenues comparable to economic damage done,
their revenue potential is similarly huge. The damage estimate for Germany, for example, equals 58 percent of tax revenues there; those for Sweden and the United States exceed
tax revenues. In practice, taxes would raise much less than
this comparison suggests, since taxing environmental damage will reduce how much occurs. And once taxes reached
their final rates—in some cases, well into the next century—
revenues might gradually decline. In counterpoint, conventional taxes on work and investment could fall at first but
would eventually have to rise again. Since taxes have long
fluctuated at this slow tempo, the adjustment stresses would
not be high by historical standards.[36]

In fiscal and environmental impacts, tax or permit systems that effectively addressed one problem, carbon emissions, would loom over all others. If the price of carbon emissions started at $22.50 per ton and gradually climbed over 50
years to $250 a ton, global emissions would roughly stabilize

through the middle of the twenty-first century and nearly halt by 2100, according to a survey of five economic models by the Energy Modeling Forum at Stanford University. (The results would be the same whether the price rise was caused by a tax or a permit system.) For comparison, a $250-per-ton tax would add 18 cents to the pump price of a liter of gasoline (69 cents for a gallon) if fully passed on to consumers. It would double the price of natural gas, and increase that of coal sixfold. Meanwhile, prices for wind, solar, geothermal, and biomass energy sources would change little. Overall, the carbon tax would probably squeeze coal out of the global energy economy, encourage efficient use of natural gas and oil, and stoke demand for renewable sources. Climate models suggest that the amount of carbon dioxide in the air would stabilize at about 65 percent above pre-industrial levels.[37]

A U.S. gas tax could fund a payroll tax cut big enough to give most workers a 6 percent raise.

According to the models, revenues would peak midway through the next century at $0.7–1.8 trillion. If all were used to cut other taxes, the world economy would grow only 0.04 percentage points less each year than otherwise (some models predict more growth, others less). The growth figures would be higher if they included estimates of the economic *benefits* of averted warming, such as reduced flooding of coastal cities and less-perturbed growing conditions in the world's breadbaskets. And since climatologists believe that significant warming could still occur in this scenario, starting the carbon tax even higher or increasing it faster could be worth the extra climate risk protection.[38]

Tax and permit systems have begun to take root in environmental policies around the world. But the collection of those in place today is patchy, and inadequate to some of the most serious problems we face. If market-based approaches are to go from novelty to mainstay, policymakers around the world need to learn quickly from these experiences and then apply them to the full gamut of environmental problems.

Out of the fertile ground of experience, mature trunks of environmental and fiscal policy will then grow. One mark of that maturity will be a healthy respect for not only the potential of the new approach, but its limitations.

When to Tax, When to Regulate

Taxes and regulations are often cast as polar opposites. Regulatory approaches, born out of environmentalists' distrust of businesses, are the bad old policies, or so the fable runs. The best way to make sure firms cleaned up was to tell companies exactly how to do it. But now regulations have become burdensomely complex and perverse, wasting businesses' money and often failing to protect the environment as well. Tax and permit systems are the coming fashion. They can sweep away the tangle of rules, freeing business from its regulatory shackles.

Like most fables, this one contains some truth. Most of the bricks in the environmental policy edifice built during the last 30 years have been fired from the stuff of legal codes, not tax codes. And to be sure, governments have often overstretched regulation, and barely tapped the potential of market approaches. But the full truth is that the two approaches are best seen as complements, not rivals. Elegant in theory, tax and permit systems rarely work so neatly in practice. And less-pretty regulations have done much environmental good. Making the industrial economy operate efficiently within environmental limits will require synthesizing the two approaches, using the strengths of each to compensate for the weaknesses of the other.

Environmental regulations on the books have scored important successes. In Western Europe, for example, regulators can point to a 47 percent reduction in sulfur emissions between 1970 and 1993, due substantially to rules requiring scrubbers in coal plants. In the United States, tightened tailpipe emissions standards for new cars and light trucks made catalytic converters universal over the same time span, cutting NO_x emissions 6 percent, carbon monoxide 33 percent, and volatile organic compounds (smog ingredients) 54 percent, all despite a 44 percent increase in driving.[39]

Moreover non-market approaches will continue to be essential to protecting the public interest. Laws—not market forces alone—are what will protect endangered species, manage nuclear waste, and ban pollutants that may be deemed unacceptable in any amount, such as DDT or dioxins. Waste incinerators, as long as they are built, are likely to be disproportionately located in poor and minority neighborhoods unless these communities have the legal means to protect themselves.

There is little evidence that regulations have hurt businesses or chased them into "pollution havens."

Contrary to popular belief, there is remarkably little evidence that regulations have seriously depressed the fortunes of industry, or that they have chased businesses into "pollution havens"—countries with lax environmental rules. For example, between 1970 and 1990, U.S. industries making and exporting the most pollution-intensive products such as paper and chemicals—all big spenders on regulation-required pollution control—fared better as a group in global competition than less-polluting industries, according to Robert Repetto, an economist at the World Resources Institute in Washington, D.C. A 1992 World Bank literature survey concluded that "the many empirical studies which have attempted to test these hypotheses [of regulatory harm] have shown no evidence to support them."[40]

Moreover, debates over the costs of regulation have also often obscured their societal benefits, such as lower medical bills thanks to cleaner air. One study that has analyzed the benefits, also led by Repetto, found them to be substantial for some industries. Regulations were one reason the U.S. electric utility industry, for instance, spent 8 percent more for the amount of power sold in 1991 than it did in 1970. But once the economic benefits of less air pollution were factored in—an unorthodox but essential step in understanding the economics of regulation—this apparent productivity decline turned into an 8–15 percent productivity increase from the point of view of society as a whole. And more fundamentally, though less quantifiably, the regulations nudged the country closer to the ideal of the society that respects the right to a healthy environment.[41]

Regulations sometimes even benefit polluters. The prod of new pollution rules often stimulates companies to change and innovate, making them more, not less, competitive, argues Michael Porter of the Harvard Business School, who has studied dozens of examples. Searching for ways to cut resource waste, some managers have discovered ways to cut financial waste—or create new products. Executives at Rhone-Poulenc in Chalampe, France, discovered just such a connection when air pollution rules forced them to install $12 million worth of equipment to recover diacids, byproducts of nylon-making, rather than incinerate them. They now earn $3 million a year selling the chemicals as dye and tanning additives and coagulation agents, a handsome return on investment.[42]

Nevertheless, regulations are increasingly being pushed beyond their limits. Because they often focus on means rather than ends, they tend to discourage innovation. And though they may work well when there is a front-runner solution (such as catalytic converters), they tend to break down in the face of complexity. A joint EPA-Amoco Corporation study documented one telling absurdity at the oil company's Yorktown, Virginia, refinery. Regulations required Amoco to spend $31 million on a wastewater treatment plant to stop airborne emissions of benzene, a carcinogen. Meanwhile, the rules failed to cover benzene emissions from a nearby loading dock—which could have been reduced as much for just $6 million. As one exasperated refinery official put it, "Give us a goal to meet rather than all the regulations.... That worked in the 1970's, when the pollution problems were much more visible and simpler. It's not working now."[43]

The growing use of environmental tax and permit systems is one response to that plea. Whenever environmental goals can be expressed in a single number—how many tons of benzene should be permitted into an airshed each year, for example, or how much water pumped from an aquifer—and whenever actual pollution or depletion rates can be estimated, market mechanisms offer an alternative. Such quantifiable problems include: urban smog; acid rain; overfishing; depletion and pollution of ground and surface water; and emissions of airborne toxics, ozone-depleting chemicals, and greenhouse gases. And as the state of New Jersey has shown, market mechanisms can also supplement regulations in the more complex tasks of managing ecosystems and planning land use.

Thus tax and permit systems seem to offer all the benefits of regulations without the disadvantages. They allow governments to do what they do best—set targets for reducing environmental damage—while letting the market do what it does best—find the cheapest ways to get there. And many of the defenses of regulation—based on the often minimal harm to competitiveness, the economic benefits, the ability to stimulate innovation—apply at least as well to market-based approaches.

But taxes are not instant cures for environmental ailments. For instance, low-density zoning laws and heavy highway spending often give people little choice but to drive. To the extent that this happens (and to the extent that they already drive small cars), taxing gas does not so much discourage gas use as punish it. If governments of sprawl-afflicted countries such as the United States and Australia want gas tax hikes to work well, and fairly, they will need to give people better alternatives to driving. They will need to spend more on mass transit, as much of Western Europe already does, and rewrite zoning laws to foster neighborhoods that more intimately mix schools, homes, and shops. Together, these changes can lure people from behind the wheel and onto sidewalks, bike paths, or bus lines.[44]

Another shortcoming of the pure market approach is that the environmental problems sometimes defy measurement, making it difficult to apply quotas or taxes. As a result, governments often have to tax rough proxies for actual pollution. Sweden, for example, taxes fertilizer sales rather than the amount of fertilizer that drains into surface and ground water, since that would be impractical to gauge. The exhaust spewing unmonitored from millions of cars provides another classic example. During annual car inspections, governments could perform odometer readings and emissions tests and use them to at least estimate a car's pollution over the past year, providing a rough base for a tax.[45]

Unfortunately, the more policymakers latch onto what is easiest to measure rather than most relevant (like the man who looked for his keys near the lamppost because that was where he could see the sidewalk), the less effective taxes become. Often, the best idea is to call non-market approaches to the assistance of market approaches, as World Bank economist Gunnar Eskeland found during detailed studies of pollution control in Chile, Mexico, and Indonesia. In Mexico City, one of the world's most smog-burdened cities, administrative expense and corruption make it nearly impossible to institute taxes based on annual car inspections. The practical palliative, he concluded, would be to require catalytic converters in new cars. But while converters can dramatically lower emissions per kilometer driven, they do nothing to reduce driving. That is where the gas tax comes in.[46]

Regulations can also lower other barriers to tax and permit effectiveness. Even with today's low energy prices, for instance, consumers and companies often miss opportunities to save money by investing in energy-efficient appliances. Evidently, they do not respond to market signals nearly as nimbly as economists would wish. Regulations can help make the decisions for them, by blocking off the most wasteful options. For example, efficiency standards adopted in the United States during the last 10 years on refrigerators, fluorescent lights, and other appliances have pushed the average efficiency of new models up sharply, and will eventually save households an average $250 a year. If governments taxed energy or carbon emissions, that would only make efficiency standards more valuable in shunting consumers away from the most energy-guzzling equipment.[47]

Along with regulations, other government programs can work synergistically with environmental taxes. The taxes can even provide the funding for such efforts. The Swedish government, for example, credits the dramatic drop in fertilizer use during the 1980s both to the taxes on fertilizer sales and to education programs, funded by the new revenues, that raised farmers' awareness of the financial and environmental costs of overuse.[48]

Environmental policymakers need to resist the temptation to throw out the old when they bring in the new. The problems at hand are grave, demanding hard-headed, practical decisionmaking. If regulations or other programs have something to offer, then they should be used, in place of or in addition to tax and permit systems. Market-based policies will work best if the signals they send are orchestrated with policies across the entire apparatus of government.

Dealing a Fair Hand

Tax and permit systems are like power saws. In the hands of a skilled carpenter, they can vastly facilitate the task of making economies environmentally sustainable. But when not handled with care, they can quickly tear through planks in the social structure, or slice into human flesh. Creating an economy that does not undermine its environmental foundation will require some radical restructuring. Some people, such as low-income families and coal miners, will have a particularly hard time making the transition. Others, such as traditional fishers in waters recently over-exploited by newcomers, stand at risk of bearing the costs of others' short-sightedness. If the overarching goal of environmental policy is to allow future generations to meet their basic needs, it seems inconsistent to make it harder for people today to do the same.

Low-income consumers are one group that can have particular difficulty adapting to environmental tax hikes. They usually spend disproportionately high shares of their income on energy, water, and resource-intensive products, whose prices would likely be lifted by environmental taxes. In the United States, for example, a $100-per-ton carbon tax on fossil fuels (equivalent to 7 cents per liter of gasoline and 27 cents per gallon) would take only 2.3 percent of the spending budgets of the richest 10 percent of households, but 3.7 percent among the poorest 10 percent, making it "regressive." And within this poorest tenth, elderly pensioners in the northern half of the country, who need the most heat, would spend even more. In developing countries, the urban poor could also be hit hard. Manila provides a representative example: the richest fifth of households devote 5 percent of their income to energy, while the poorest fifth spend 12 percent. (Many of the rural poor in developing countries still operate largely outside the market economy, collecting their own water and fuel, so they might hardly notice environmental taxes.)[49]

Policymakers can mitigate environmental tax regressivity in several ways. First, they can adjust the tax code itself. The coastal town of Setúbal, Portugal, recently took this approach when it "terraced" its new water taxes. Households can buy 25 cubic meters a month tax-free, enough to meet most basic needs; but above that threshold, the levy kicks in, rising in three stages. The Netherlands did the same with the new duties on natural gas and power in 1996. In addition, it increased the standard income tax deductions, especially for senior citizens, and lowered the tax rate on the lowest income bracket. As a result, most low-income people came out just about where they started.[50]

Governments can also compensate for regressivity through other programs. They can help the poor pay their heating bills, cut those bills by putting insulation and efficient heaters into their homes, and expand bus service in low-income neighborhoods. In many Southern European cities, short heating seasons and convenient mass transit already combine to reduce energy costs for the poor. As a

result, energy and carbon taxes there would tend to be progressive rather than regressive, taking proportionally more
from the better-off. Finally, governments can also assist low-
income consumers with unrelated expenses such as food. In
general, these measures will reach distinct but overlapping
populations, so they need to be combined carefully to reach
as many people as possible.[51]

Policymakers can also use the flexibility of tax and permit systems to minimize the costs they can impose on people who make a living extracting resources. In New Zealand,
indigenous Maori had been fishing for centuries before west-
erners began fishing there too in the 1930s. After World War
II, larger boats became more common and total catch shot
up, leading to overfishing by the 1970s. When the government put fisheries under permit trading systems in 1986, it
based allocations on how much each fisher had caught in
the early 1980s. Since total catch had to be scaled back—up
to 80 percent for some species—many Maori received shares
too small to live on, despite their ancestral claims.
Meanwhile, relative newcomers ended up ahead of where
they had started a few decades earlier. Fortunately for the
Maori, they could turn to the courts, where they fought successfully to increase their permanent allocations in 1989
and 1992.[52]

A different divide emerged after the U.S. government
launched its first fishing permit systems in the early 1990s,
off the coast of Alaska: not between traditional fishers and
newcomers, but between boat owners and boat workers. The
government gave all $800 million worth of permits to boat
owners. Boat workers, who would seem to have some claim
to the windfall generated by local resources, received none.
Since then, the industry has moved toward large, automated trawlers, which support fewer and lower-paying jobs.
Control of much of the fish resource and earnings from it
have effectively been transferred from local communities to
investors elsewhere. The government might have avoided
this outcome if it had allocated some permits to boat workers, who could then have sold or rented them to boat own-

ers. Or it could have auctioned the permits and passed the revenue back to local communities, much as Alaska already does with its oil royalties.[53]

For all the conflict they generate, these permit schemes work mainly to preserve the fishing industry in its present form. But if humanity is to create an industrial society in which people do not injure each other and their descendants simply by getting up and going to work each day, other businesses need to be revolutionized. A sustainable economy will still need paper, chemicals, and steel, but makers of these products will have to find ways to pollute less and recycle more. To date, industries have proved remarkably adaptable in the face of tightening environmental requirements. There is nevertheless an unavoidable tension between the need to make major changes and the desire to minimize the pain of adjustment. A handful of industries may need to disappear altogether. It will be nearly impossible, for example, to get carbon emissions down to levels needed for climate stability without phasing out most of the coal industry.[54]

International trade pressures can make it even harder for nations to begin the process of change. A country that levies a stiff carbon tax, for example, may end up sending steel and chemical makers abroad rather than lowering their emissions. The local economy then loses while the global environment gains nothing. This is why the carbon taxes in the Nordic countries and the Netherlands, all small nations heavily dependent on trade, provide exemptions for industry, and why, worldwide, most energy taxes fall primarily on consumers.[55]

The ironic upshot of such concessions is that the most polluting industries are taxed least. A more precise way to strike the balance is to apply "border corrections" to environmental taxes. This entails rebating taxes on exports and taxing imports as if they had been made domestically. The United States took this approach when it backed its duty on ozone-depleting substances with import duties on products made with or containing the chemicals.[56]

The biggest potential obstacles to border corrections are international free trade agreements such as the

Maastricht Treaty, which created the European Union (EU), and the General Agreement on Tariffs and Trade, which set up the World Trade Organization (WTO). Both treaties work to prohibit protectionism, but are ambiguous on border corrections for environmental taxes. The European Commission, the administrative arm of the European Union government, has set an important precedent by approving Danish carbon tax rebates for energy-intensive industries, even as it acknowledged that they apparently contravened EU trade laws. Similarly, in 1994, the WTO's predecessor court upheld the U.S. "gas guzzler" tax even though it mostly affected inefficient Japanese- and European-made luxury cars. It argued that the tax was intended to protect the environment, not restrain trade. Nevertheless, the conventional wisdom is that the WTO will eventually prove unfriendly to border corrections.[57]

A sustainable economy will need paper, chemicals, and steel, but makers will have to pollute less and recycle more.

In the long run, the best solution would be for trading partners to avoid competitiveness concerns by harmonizing environmental tax and permit systems, especially when they address international problems such as acid rain and global warming. An international forum in which such tax changes could be negotiated and coordinated, perhaps operating under the auspices of the WTO or the U.N. Commission on Sustainable Development, could therefore speed progress. But until economic superpowers such as Germany, Japan, and the United States confront the carbon problem, for example, the freedom of small, pioneering countries to apply border corrections will be crucial to the development of carbon taxes worldwide.[58]

Even if countries secure the freedom to use border corrections, many industries will still have a hard time making the transition to environmental sustainability, particularly ones that operate right at the interface between the economy and the environment, such as the oil, minerals, and timber industries. Their operations often dot rural landscapes and company towns sprout up around them. As these industries go, so go many of the regional economies they support. For investors, that may mean lost profits. Worse, for workers, it may mean lost jobs. A diverse urban economy can heal quickly after the loss of a single industry, but rural economies recover less easily. Many workers may be forced to choose between long-term joblessness and moving away. Squeezed between the industrial status quo and environmental limits, they will find little consolation in knowing that the rest of the economy will benefit in the long run.

The costs of the tax-spurred transition to sustainability must be taken seriously, but they can be minimized. Indeed, the sooner the transition begins, the more gradual, orderly, and painless it can be. And by stimulating employment and investment in more environmentally supportable industries, simultaneous cuts in conventional taxes can further smooth the process of change. Many workers in the few dying sectors would have time to retrain, perhaps with government assistance, and move to newly invigorated industries such as solar energy, steel recycling, and ecotourism.

Tax Reform for a Sustainable Society

As mindful as policymakers should be of the side effects of environmental tax shifting, they should not lose sight of the great benefits for society as a whole, particularly for investors and workers on the winning side of a tax shift. Consumers and companies may spend less on environmentally insupportable products—but that will leave them more to spend on environmentally sound ones. For every declining coal industry, there will be a rising solar industry. For every discarded, polluting production process, a cleaner alternative will be adopted. Since the changes will run deep, the economic opportunities will be huge.

Among potential environmental tax and permit systems, those aimed at reducing carbon emissions will likely affect the global economy and environment most. The Framework Convention on Climate Change, signed in 1992 at the Rio "Earth Summit," set up legal and political machinery for coordinating international efforts to stop climate change. But follow-up negotiations since have not put much meat on these bones. Whatever agreements are eventually reached will probably set forth how fast the global carbon pie should shrink and how it should be divided. Western industrial countries might agree to one reduction schedule, and formerly communist and developing countries to a separate, slower one. The Montreal Protocol, which is orchestrating phase-outs of ozone-depleting chemicals, follows a similar plan.[59]

For every declining coal industry, there will be a rising solar industry.

Once a schedule was agreed upon, tradable permit systems might provide ideal tools for governments needing to keep their economies operating within agreed limits. Each country could auction its permits domestically and use the revenues to cut other taxes. Electric utilities would have to buy enough to cover emissions from their coal-fired power plants, and oil companies would need to do the same for gasoline they sold to drivers. Taking the permit approach further, economists have argued that allowing companies to trade permits *across* national borders could substantially cut the cost of climate protection. A Mexican company, for example, could then earn credits by planting trees and sell them to a Texas utility for less than the utility would otherwise have to spend scrapping its coal plants. The same amount of carbon would be sequestered, but at lower cost.[60]

Integrating trading systems across borders, though sensible, does not resolve the tough issue at the heart of the climate negotiations: how emission rights will initially be distributed among nations. Developing countries have argued that they should get most of the pollution rights since they are home to 80 percent of the world's people, yet have emitted only 20 percent of the carbon from fossil fuel burning to date. Industrial countries would then have to buy billions of tons worth of permits from poorer countries in order to keep their coal plants and cars running, generating a trillion-dollar cash transfer. The U.N. Development Programme has put the case this way: "Such flows would be neither aid nor charity. They would be the outcome of a free market mechanism that penalizes the richer nations' overconsumption of the global commons." Such a huge transfer of wealth seems unlikely. Yet what seems equally improbable is that rising carbon emitters like China would abide an arrangement that gave industrial countries most of the quota in the future simply because they have emitted most in the past. The most likely deal is a compromise between these two extremes.[61]

Internationally coordinated tax regimes might also play a role. Since 1992, the European Commission has put forward a series of proposals for a tax on carbon emissions and energy use for EU members. In all of its incarnations, the tax would rise slowly over many years, with the revenues used to cut other taxes within each country. So far, all the proposals have foundered against opposition from the United Kingdom, and to a lesser extent from southern European countries that fear the tax will put some of their industries at a competitive disadvantage against their northern neighbors. If the political winds change, an EU tax regime could eventually emerge from this protracted debate. It could work well under a global climate treaty as long as tax rates were periodically adjusted to keep emission reductions on course.[62]

Along with the high-profile carbon issue, environmental problems ranging from groundwater depletion to toxic air pollution seem destined for increasing treatment with market-based policies. Ideally, each charge or permit regime will be adopted over appropriate geographic scales. Tax levels or permit caps aimed at smog prevention, for example, would vary from city to city. But those for reducing acid rain would be applied regionally or internationally. Meanwhile, subsidies for activities with major environmental side effects would be radically cut back.

These developments would create thousands of business opportunities for companies offering environmentally sound products and services. Consumer pressure, regulations, and even a few taxes are already giving a taste of what may come. The phase-out of CFCs, for example, is creating billion-dollar markets for chemical alternatives along with refrigerators and air conditioners designed to use them. Sales of organic food grew 13-fold in the United States between 1980 and 1994, from $180 million to $2.3 billion. They grew similarly in the European Union. Global windpower capacity climbed 1,290 megawatts in 1996, nearly four times the rise four years earlier, with Germany and India installing the most. The latest doubling of global solar cell sales took six years. The international market for "environmental" goods and services that monitor and control pollution, recycle, and conserve energy is today far larger, amounting to roughly $408 billion in 1994, and projected to reach $572 billion by 2001. (See Table 2.)[63]

TABLE 2

Global Market for Environmental Protection Goods and Services, 1994, with Projection for 2001

Region	Sales 1994	2001
	(billion dollars)	
North America	176	233
Latin America	7	15
Western Europe	127	168
Eastern Europe, Russia	6	11
Africa	2	4
Middle East	4	6
Australia, New Zealand, Japan	72	92
Developing Asia	14	43
World	408	572

Source: See endnote 63.

With comprehensive environmental taxation, the global economy will eventually evolve into a configuration whose outlines we can already draw, but whose details are too complicated to envision. Flows of resources into and out of the economy—materials, energy, nutrients, waste, and pollution—would slow to rates compatible with the health of people and the earth. People would draw renewable energy from the sun or the earth's hot interior; wood, fruit, and rattan from sustainably managed forests; and water from sustainably managed rivers and aquifers. Economies would be reengineered to *minimize* the production of goods—but maximize the services provided by them. Builders would insulate homes so well that the inhabitants' own bodies would generate much of the heat in winter. Buses and refrigerators would be designed for easy repair, disassembly, and recycling. Much as a tree's fallen leaves become food for molds, so would one factory's waste would become another's feedstock, making the concept of pollution nearly obsolete. Industries that made intensive use of human skills but minimal use of depletable resources would prosper.[64]

Taxes alone will not create a sustainable society. To control population, access to birth control will need to be made universal. Governments will also need to step up programs that increase literacy, education, and economic independence of women in order to reduce their dependence on multiple sons for social security. Land use will need to be planned and mass transit provided to yield more mobility and access with fewer cars. But because tax and permit systems directly address one crux of the environmental problem—the mismatch between individual and collective interests—it is hard to imagine how humanity can achieve sustainability without them.[65]

Tax Cuts

Unlike other environmental policies, environmental taxes raise money. This distinctive trait brings an important new dimension to environmental protection. Fully used, environmental tax and permit systems can raise trillions of dollars over the coming decades, allowing significant tax cuts for work and investment. As a result, it seems likely that governments can take major strides toward sustainability without hurting their economies in the short run. Indeed, a handful of countries have already begun to make just this sort of tax shift.

There is little question that conventional taxes on work and investment hurt economies. In the United States, according to modeling by Dale Jorgenson and Yun Kun-Young at Harvard University, the $535 billion raised in payroll taxes in 1993 cut output $158 billion (2.6 percent of GDP), as high labor costs deterred companies from expanding, or low after-tax wages discouraged people from working. The government cycled the $535 billion back into the economy through social security checks and other expenditures, but the $158 billion loss was permanent. Taxes on personal and corporate income, capital gains, retail sales, and property decreased GDP by another $373 billion (6.0 percent). Like Shylock in Shakespeare's *Merchant of Venice*, who would have taken a pound of his enemy's flesh from "nearest his heart," conventional taxes exact a toll both through how much they take and what they take it from.[66]

Though taxes are lower in developing countries, they may reduce economic production more per dollar raised. Broad-based taxes on income and profits there tend to be impractical or ineffective because most incomes are low and unrecorded, and because widespread corruption often impedes enforcement. As a result, a typical 3 percent of the population in developing countries pay income tax, compared to 60–80 percent in industrial ones. Instead (though generalizations are dangerous) developing-country governments get more of their revenue from taxes on trade and sales of certain products, particularly easy-to-track imports like machine tools. (See Table 3.) Fewer taxpayers means that efforts to implement the taxes and audit the implementers can be more concentrated and effective. Unfortunately, tax base narrowing distorts and slows economic development by causing underinvestment in industries where tax evasion happens to be easy, and overinvestment in ones where it is hard.[67]

Fortuitously, some of the most lucrative environmental taxes also apply to small groups of taxpayers, such as power companies or oil refineries. Shifting toward environmental taxation, then, may be a practical way for developing countries to reduce the economic and health damage wrought by pollution without hurting their economies. They would not be the first to take this tack. Southern Europe's culture of tax evasion drives its heavy reliance on difficult-to-dodge gas taxes.[68]

In general, though, evasion and bribery distort tax codes much less in western industrial countries than in developing ones. And with a different tax context come different tax-cutting priorities. Industrial countries use broad-based levies on corporate profits and capital gains to tax physical capital, and payroll levies to tax labor. Their personal income and sales (or value added) taxes apply to both, but mostly to labor. Under an environmental tax shift, any of these could be cut. Like the dichotomy between environmental taxes and regulations, that between taxes on physical capital and on labor is often overplayed. Many economists and business executives argue that the best way to create more and better-paying jobs is to cut capital gains or corporate profits taxes. In direct contradiction, labor groups argue that if governments want to increase payrolls they should cut payroll taxes.[69]

The truth lies in between. What distinguishes rich countries from poor ones is the quality of both their physical capital and their workforce. Just as spending on factories and rail lines is an investment in an economy's future, so is spending on education: it is an investment in *human* capital, making workers more valuable in the long run. Where taxing profits makes physical investment less worthwhile, taxing wages makes education investment less worthwhile, by reducing

TABLE 3

Tax Revenue, Total and by Source, Selected Countries, 1994

Country	Total Revenue		Sources[1]		
	Per Person	Share of GDP	Profits, Wages, and Income[2]	Sales and Trade[3]	Property
	(dollars per year[4])	(percent)	(percent share of total tax revenue)		
Germany	7,512	39	69	29	3
United States	7,040	28	70	18	12
Japan	6,235	28	73	16	12
Russia	1,621	37	58[5]	30[5]	12[5,6]
Thailand[7]	1,202	17	34	62	3[6]
Brazil[7]	1,136	18	66	29	7[6]
India[7]	121	9	58	37	4[6]

[1]Some rows do not total 100 percent because of rounding. [2]Includes employee and employer contributions to social security funds. [3]Includes taxes on turnover, sales, and value added, on specific products, and on imports and exports. [4]Converted from domestic currencies on the basis of purchasing-power parities. [5]Data for 1993. [6]Includes other taxes, and, for Russia, nontax revenue. [7]Central government only.

Source: See endnote 67.

post-graduation pay. And just as investment in factories creates opportunities for workers, investment in human capital creates opportunities for businesses. A skilled work force is one reason Intel can consider putting a new chip plant in South Korea, but not Vietnam. A healthy economy therefore needs steady investment in both computer plants and computer engineers, both tools and people. Taxes on either part of the economic dynamo hurt both.[70]

In western industrial countries, then, the tax-cut question becomes this: Which seem more underused today, machines or workers? The answer seems fairly clearly to be workers. In the United States, the economy is placing less and less value on laborers with minimal skills, causing their wages to decline. Partly as a result, 10.6 percent of families that have children and at least one full-time worker lived below the poverty line in 1995, up from 8.3 percent in 1975, for a total of 3.35 million families. And millions more struggle just above the poverty line. In Western Europe, meanwhile, stronger unions, labor laws, or traditions of lifetime employment seem to be protecting jobholders against wage pressure. But like a squeezed balloon, labor markets there are finding other ways to release pressures building on them. Wages held high by well-organized workers seem to be spurring employers to move abroad, automate, or simply not expand. As a result, the unemployment rate in the European Union climbed from 2.6 percent in 1973 to 10.9 percent in 1996, accounting for 18.1 million people. (See Figure 3.) Here, too, the problem is concentrated among less-skilled workers.[71]

The millions of families tallied by these statistics suffer most from these trends; but society as whole loses too. Unemployment and falling wages are widening the divide between haves and have-nots. In some countries, the trend is already breeding racism against immigrants, political extremism, and pessimism among young adults stuck outside the workforce. In the long run it threatens the sense of societal commonality needed to bind democracies together.[72]

Debate rages over the causes of these trends. In the United States, immigrants willing to accept low wages are often blamed—yet European countries allowing far less immigration suffer from the same pressures. Capital mobility and trade-induced competition from workers in poorer countries also play roles, though perhaps less than many suppose. In the United States, for example, wages have fallen as rapidly in industries immune to foreign competition, such as construction. Another leading theory is that new information technologies, unlike the automation technologies of 50 years ago that created a huge industrial appetite for assembly-line labor, are making much low-skilled labor obsolete. The automated teller industry has created jobs for skilled engineers but eliminated them for bank tellers.[73]

FIGURE 3

Working Families in Poverty, United States, 1975–95, and Unemployment, European Union, 1973–96

Source: See endnote 71.

And taxes contribute. Wage taxation has been rising in almost all industrial countries in recent decades. Between 1970 and 1994, taxes' claim on labor earnings climbed from 30 to 41 percent in Germany, from 18 to 26 percent in Japan, and from 20 to 24 percent in the United States. And most of those increases occurred through rises in flat-rate charges that fund social programs, not in progressive income taxes. Taxation of profits and capital gains, which accrue mostly to rich people, fell meanwhile. Economic studies have been reasonably consistent in concluding that the tax shift toward wages has added to unemployment. One study found that wage tax increases explained 0.5 percentage points of the unemployment rise in France between 1956–66 and 1980–83, 1.3 points in Canada, and 2.0 in the United Kingdom.[74]

Thus if policymakers want to boost demand for workers, the revenues from environmental levies would best be used to reverse the wage tax rise. In the United States, most of the tax cut would translate into higher paychecks, increasing rewards for investment in people. In Western Europe, more of the savings would go to businesses. But cutting the cost of employees to employers could stimulate job creation. Studies also suggest that paring down wage taxes in a way that made them more consistent with personal income taxes—grading them so that the rates fell toward zero for the lowest-paid workers—would create the most jobs. Demand would rise most for the least-skilled service workers. who are having the most trouble finding jobs.[75]

Economic models, the best tool for predicting the effects of such shifts, generally show modest but significant benefits for workers. A study by the European Commission estimated that levying a carbon/energy tax equivalent to $10 per barrel of oil and using it to pay for an across-the-board wage tax cut could create 1.5 million jobs net in the European Union, reducing unemployment 0.9 percentage points. (Some environmentally damaging industries would shed jobs.) Modeling by Jorgenson and colleagues found that a tax shift in the United States, differing in detail, would improve economic welfare fairly evenly across the income spectrum, but slightly more at the bottom.[76]

Of course these models caricature reality. They predict how much a tax cut for physical capital could boost physical investment, for example, but they often ignore the encouragement a wage tax cut would give to investment in human capital—encouragement that could be as substantial as it is hard to model. Also elusive is how much environmental taxes will stimulate innovation, allowing companies to adapt without shutting down operations and laying off workers. Nor are the reduced medical bills due to cleaner air counted, nor the potential economic benefits of less extreme weather and avoided sea level rise. On the other hand, by focusing on averages, many of the models gloss over the adjustment costs for coal miners and low-income energy consumers.[77]

TABLE 4

Tax Shifts from Work and Investment to Environmental Damage

Country, Year Initiated	Taxes Cut On	Taxes Raised On	Revenue Shifted[1] (percent)
Sweden, 1991	Personal income	Carbon and sulfur emissions	1.9
Denmark, 1994	Personal income	Motor fuel, coal, electricity, and water sales; waste incineration and landfilling; motor vehicle ownership	2.5
Spain, 1995	Wages	Motor fuel sales	0.2
Denmark, 1996	Wages, agricultural property	Carbon emissions; pesticide, chlorinated solvent, and battery sales	0.5
Netherlands, 1996	Personal income and wages	Natural gas and electricity sales	0.8
United Kingdom 1996–97	Wages	Landfilling	0.2

[1]Expressed relative to tax revenue raised by all levels of government.

Source: See endnote 78.

Since 1991, five European countries have begun to put the theory of environmental tax shifting into practice. Sweden enacted the first shift in 1991, putting $2.4 billion from new carbon and sulfur taxes, equal to 1.9 percent of all tax revenues, toward cutting income taxes. As concern grew over unemployment in Europe, later shifts, in Denmark, the Netherlands, Spain, and the United Kingdom, focused more on cutting wage taxes. (See Table 4.) Unfortunately, it will be difficult for analysts to discern the effects of such small adjustments in complex and constantly evolving economies. Only a much larger tectonic shift within national tax codes would generate enough jobs to show up on economists' seismographs.[78]

In the end, the greatest economic benefit of tax shifting will come from the environmental tax increases themselves. The tax cuts are a bonus that can compensate the immediate costs of environmental protection—and then some. Tax shifting will not make economic miracles in poor countries nor end unemployment and wage declines in rich ones. But it can help. Even if 18 million new jobs are needed, 1.5 million more would still be a blessing for 1.5 million families and their communities. Worthy ends in themselves, the additional benefits also open up new avenues for building political support for a tax shift—support that could be crucial to achieving environmental sustainability.

The Political Challenge

Modeling the century-long effects of powerful policy instruments like taxes on economies and the environment is ultimately an exercise one step this side of soothsaying. But persevering economists do have one advantage over policymakers. They can halve or double a carbon tax, for example, at the touch of a few keys; any policymaker who tries to move so quickly will encounter the political fight of a lifetime. Under an environmental tax-shifting plan, every penny raised in new taxes would be returned through cuts in other taxes, and society would be better off overall. But these changes are certain to arouse opposition from the highly influential groups that will lose out at least in the short term. Mapping a route through this rocky political terrain to a sustainable society will not be easy.

An imbalance limiting the scope of most environmental taxes stems from the fact that the people who stand to lose from them, such as environmentally destructive businesses, are generally much better organized and financed than those who stand to gain—including the general public. For politicians, charging for pollution or resource use has often meant going out on a limb: on one side they have faced adamant industry opposition; on the other, a poorly informed public. When President Bill Clinton proposed an energy tax in 1993, its costs were clear to those who would pay it, but since it was to be used to cut the budget deficit, its benefits were much fuzzier, even to the sharpest economists. Political support for the tax was thus weak. Major manufacturers and energy producers launched a multimillion-dollar lobbying campaign against the tax—the largest such effort ever mounted to stop a bill in U.S. history—and discovered a President quick to compromise. Many voters also disliked the Clinton bill. But tellingly, the only scrap of it that survived the congressional battle was a 1.1-cent-per-liter (4.3-cent-per-gallon) gasoline and diesel tax, coming largely out of the pockets of consumers, not businesses.[79]

Political factors can cut both ways, not only blocking new environmental taxes, but leading to over-reliance on old ones. In some cases, recipients of environmental tax revenues become so vested in them that they work to stimulate with one hand what they tax with the other. In the United States, for instance, local forest service offices are allowed to keep a share of the proceeds from the timber they sell, an arrangement that has been found to accelerate logging. Off the coast of Alaska, fishing industry pressure seems to be behind the regulating agency's decision to give away enough permits to allow over-fishing. Onshore, Alaska residents have become accustomed to receiving $1,000 checks every October from the state government, their share of the royalties from oil production in Prudhoe Bay. Some recipients have argued that the state should pay lobbyists in Washington, D.C., to press for drilling in ecologically sensitive areas in order to boost future royalties.[80]

Taxes on pollution seem less vulnerable to such environmentally harmful distortions. There is little sign, for example, that Western European governments have built roads in order to raise the take from their large gas taxes. In the Netherlands, declines in water pollution led water authorities to *increase* pollution taxes in order maintain revenue, causing further pollution reductions.[81]

In lobbying for new taxes, what has sometimes worked politically is to earmark the revenues for spending on industries that pay them, or, more rarely, on environmental protection programs. Water taxes in France, for example, cycle back to polluters as subsidies for investing in pollution reduction. Giving valuable permits to polluting industries, rather than auctioning them, has a similar effect. Earmarking funds for environmental protection agencies can be especially useful in developing countries where such agencies are underfunded. It can also win over voters who mistrust policymakers to spend the money wisely on their own.[82]

The Canadian province of Ontario discovered this political dynamic when it adopted a tax on fuel-inefficient vehicles in 1991. Such vehicle taxes can be particularly effective because they reach consumers just as they make one of the most important decisions affecting how much they pollute: what car to buy. But the Ontario tax, though modest, proved hugely unpopular, leading the government to scale it back and use some of the remaining revenues to subsidize the most efficient cars. The resulting tax-subsidy hybrid is the world's first "feebate" system. Efficient cars did gain market share in the early 1990s, though whether the feebates helped is not clear. What the experience has demonstrated is the political palatability of earmarking environmentally friendly taxes to pay for environmentally friendly subsidies.[83]

Subsidies and tax-subsidy combinations may make significant contributions to environmental protection, but in the long run they will hit limits. Ultimately, societies can no more subsidize their way out of environmental problems than they can make neighborhoods safe by paying burglars not to burgle. Paying people to do the right thing quickly becomes unaffordable. Sweetening the environmental tax medicine by cutting distortionary taxes will do more economic good in the long run.than adding new subsidies.[84]

A 1994 tax proposal by Greenpeace Germany exemplifies the powerful mix of ideas that has given impetus to this brand of environmental taxation in Western Europe. It envisions a tax that would push energy prices up by roughly 7 percent a year over at least 15 years. The government would pool the tax receipts taken from consumers through their utility bills and then return it all by mailing "eco bonus" checks worth a flat amount per person to every home in the country. Poorer households, which spend less than average on energy (though more as a percentage of their incomes), would gain from the system. Rich households would lose—though very slightly compared with their incomes. Similarly, industry would get its money back in the form of across-the-board payroll tax cuts, which would stimulate job creation. Total energy use would fall by the year 2010 to 14 percent below what it would be without tax reform, according to the German Institute for Economic Research, a major economic think tank in Berlin. In addition, 600,000 jobs would be generated within 10 years.[85]

Earmarking funds for environmental protection can be useful in developing countries where agencies are underfunded.

Unlike the Clinton tax, the Greenpeace proposal has exploited divisions within industry, garnered popular support, and pushed tax shifting onto the public agenda. Under this plan, industries that use the most energy and the least labor, such as chemical manufacturers, steelmakers, and coal companies—which were responsible for 46 percent of value added in private industry in 1988, but only 42 percent of employment—would see their costs rise. Cleaner, more labor-intensive industries—from education to telecommunications to retail—represented 50 percent of output and 54 of employment; they would save money, and probably expand. The automobile industry, with 4 percent of output and employment, would break even. Thus a comfortable majority of the electorate in private industry would work for companies that would break even or gain. (See Table 5.)[86]

Impressively, the proposal has won support from some major businesses and labor groups, perhaps tipping the political balance toward tax shifting in Germany. The appliance maker AEG, the Tupperware company, and a dozen other big businesses have signed on with environmentalists to fight for tax reform. Even the head of BMW has endorsed the idea, perhaps because he believes, as U.S. automakers appear to, that energy taxes will encourage consumers to invest a little extra in more energy-efficient cars. The German metal workers' union, IG-Metall, the largest union in Europe, has also voiced strong support. With employment already falling steadily in the German iron and steel industries, it is clear that the status quo offers little security for union members. Payroll tax cuts and an accelerated transition to a sustainable, more labor-intensive steel-recycling industry would do them more good. It would create more jobs—and jobs that would last. Yet major industry groups have strongly opposed tax shifting, so far successfully, arguing that any energy tax increase would only deepen the unemployment crisis. They miss the point that environmental tax reform need not increase taxes, only shift them.[87]

Identifying and organizing potential winners under a tax shift is a promising and important political strategy. But in the final analysis, the key to enacting a fundamental shift in the use of taxes is a fundamental shift in public perception of them. What has powered the modest tax shifts in Europe is the widely shared concern over both environmental and economic problems. Lobbying by service and light manufacturing industries, though promising, has yet to play a decisive role.

Educating the public requires honesty about what tax shifting can deliver and what it cannot. For one of the quickest ways to lose the support of a public already grown cynical about self-styled tax reformers is to promise more than one can deliver. Under an environmental tax shift, the biggest change most citizens will experience will not be in

TABLE 5

Selected Losers and Gainers under Greenpeace Germany Tax Shift Proposal

Industry	Share of Value Added[1]	Share of Employment[1]	Price Change[2]
	(percent)	(percent)	(percent)
Industries That Lose	45.7	42.1	—
Coal[3]	0.6	0.8	+50.7
Chemicals	3.7	2.3	+12.5
Iron and Steel	0.8	0.7	+5.0
Automobile Industry	4.1	4.1	0.0
Industries That Gain	50.1	53.8	—
Construction	3.9	4.8	–0.5
Electrical Equipment	4.5	4.8	–1.4
Postal and Telecommunications	2.6	2.2	–5.7

[1]Percentages are of private sector output and employment only, for 1988. Columns may not add to 100 percent because of rounding. [2]After 15 years of tax shift phase-in, assuming all tax costs and savings are passed on to customers. [3]For hard coal, subsidies would still exceed taxes unless phased out.

Source: See endnote 86.

how much tax they pay, but in what they are taxed for doing. Thus the questions they must be asked run along these lines: Would you rather you and your neighbors were taxed for working, or for polluting each other's lungs by driving? Only when people answer such questions in ways that make sense for society in the long run can environmental tax reform be taken to its full potential. Polling data from the United States and European Union suggest that many people are prepared to take these questions seriously. On both sides of the Atlantic, 70 percent of those surveyed have favored environmental tax shifting once they understood it.[88]

J. Andrew Hoerner, an analyst with the Environmental Tax Program in Washington, D.C., has offered a hopeful historical analogy. In 1982, two members of the U.S. Congress introduced a bill to close a slew of tax loopholes and use the savings to lower overall rates. Few took it seriously since it made enemies out of thousands of lobbyists in the capital. Yet like a legislative cat, the bill survived a half-dozen scrapes with death to become law four years later. The final act, though perfect in no one's eyes, did make the tax code fairer, creating huge winners and losers in the process, much as a major environmental tax shift would. In the end, what forced the bill forward was that tax simplification was just too compelling an idea to be denied.[89]

That reform only changed *how* governments tax the things they already tax. But major shifts in *what* they tax will also have to be carried by waves of popular support. Such support can only arise from a collective appreciation of the dangers of the current environmental paralysis and the benefits of ending it. Therein lies what may be the last, best hope for reconciling the global economy to ecological reality.

Notes

1. One in eleven U.S. children have dangerous levels of lead in their blood. See U.S. Environmental Protection Agency (EPA) and U.S. Consumer Product Safety Commission, *Protect Your Family from Lead in Your Home* (Washington, DC: EPA, 1996). One in four Iowans drink water that contains pesticides at some time during the year. See Pamela Wexler, "Iowa's 1987 Groundwater Protection Act," in Robert J.P. Gale and Stephan R. Barg, eds., *Green Budget Reform: An International Casebook of Leading Practices* (London: Earthscan, 1995). Christopher Flavin and Odil Tunali, *Climate of Hope: New Strategies for Stabilizing the World's Atmosphere,* Worldwatch Paper 130 (Washington, DC: Worldwatch Institute, June 1996).

2. Alan J. Krupnick and Dallas Bertraw, "The Social Costs of Electricity: Do the Numbers Add Up?" *Energy and Resource Economics* (in press).

3. Revenue figures are Worldwatch estimates, based on GDP and tax revenue figures for western industrial countries from Organisation for Economic Co-operation and Development (OECD), *Revenue Statistics of OECD Member Countries 1965–1995* (Paris: 1996), on GDP figures for other countries from World Bank, *World Development Report 1996* (Washington, DC: 1996), Table 12, <http://www.worldbank.org/html/iecdd/wdi96.exe>, and on central government tax revenue as a share of GDP for other countries from idem, *World Development Indicators* (Washington, DC: in press). "Taxes on work and investment" excludes land taxes, which are liberally estimated at half of total property taxes in OECD countries, and excludes energy and environmental taxes, using figures for the European Union (EU) from Commission of the European Communities (EC), Statistical Office of the European Communities (Eurostat), *Structures of the Taxation Systems in the European Union* (Luxembourg: Office for Official Publications of the European Communities (OOP), 1996), and for non-EU OECD countries from OECD, *Environmental Taxes in OECD Countries* (Paris: 1995). For non-OECD countries, land, energy, and environmental taxes are assumed to generate at most 16 percent of tax revenues, a figure that appears liberal based on International Monetary Fund (IMF), *Government Finance Statistics Yearbook 1994* (Washington, DC: 1994). All figures are for 1994, converted to dollars using market exchange rates. On subsidies, see David Malin Roodman, *Paying the Piper: Subsidies, Politics, and the Environment,* Worldwatch Paper 133 (Washington, DC: Worldwatch Institute, December 1996).

4. Ernst U. von Weizsäcker and Jochen Jesinghaus, *Ecological Tax Reform: A Policy Proposal for Sustainable Development* (London: Zed Books, 1992).

5. European information from European Environment Agency (EEA), *Environmental Taxes: Implementation and Environmental Effectiveness* (Copenhagen: 1996); U.S. polling result is based on a sample of 1,000 adults taken in January 1993 by Greenberg-Lake/The Analysis Group, Washington, DC, and The Tarrance Group, Alexandria, VA, cited in Kate Stewart, Belden

& Russonello, Washington, DC, letter to author, 10 March 1997.

6. OECD, *Environmental Taxes,* op. cit. note 3; Michel Potier, "China Charges for Pollution," *The OECD Observer,* February/March 1995; Hans Th. A. Bressers and Jeannette Schuddeboom, "A Survey of Effluent Charges and Other Economic Instruments in Dutch Environmental Policy," in OECD, *Applying Economic Instruments to Environmental Policies in OECD and Dynamic Non-member Economies* (Paris: 1994); Rory McLeod, *Market Access Issues for the New Zealand Seafood Trade* (Wellington: New Zealand Fishing Industry Board, 1996); Northern European tax shifts from P. Bohm, "Environment and Taxation: The Case of Sweden," in OECD, *Environment and Taxation: The Cases of the Netherlands, Sweden and the United States* (Paris: 1994), from Mikael Skou Andersen, "The Green Tax Reform in Denmark: Shifting the Focus of Tax Liability," *Journal of Environmental Liability* 2, no. 2 (1994), from Ministry of Housing, Spatial Planning, and Environment (VROM), *The Netherlands' Regulatory Tax on Energy: Questions and Answers* (The Hague: 1996), from Thomas Schröder, "Spain: Improve Competitiveness through an ETR," *Wuppertal Bulletin on Ecological Tax Reform* (Wuppertal, Germany: Wuppertal Institute for Climate, Environment, and Energy), summer 1995, and from "Landfill Tax Regime Takes Shape," *ENDS Report* (London: Environmental Data Services), November 1995.

7. Figure of $7.5 trillion is a Worldwatch estimate, based on OECD, *Revenue Statistics,* op. cit. note 3, on World Bank, *World Development Report,* op. cit. note. 3, Table 12, and on idem, *World Development Indicators,* op. cit. note 3.

8. Figure of $572 billion is from Environmental Business International (EBI), *The Global Environmental Market and United States Industry Competitiveness* (San Diego: 1996).

9. Arthur Cecil Pigou, *The Economics of Welfare,* 4th ed. (London: Macmillan, 1932; first published 1920), cited in Mikael Skou Andersen, *Governance by Green Taxes: Making Pollution Prevention Pay* (Manchester, U.K.: Manchester University Press, 1994); conversion to 1995 dollars based on a price index relative to 1920, from U.K. Office for National Statistics, "International Purchasing Power of the Pound," <http://www.ons.gov.uk/ukinfigs/stats/power.htm>, London, viewed 11 February 1997.

10. Ernst Ulrich von Weizsäcker, "Let Prices Tell the Ecological Truth," *Our Planet* 7, no. 1 (1995); Pigou from Andersen, op. cit. note 9.

11. Bressers and Schuddeboom, op. cit. note 6; technology development from Jan Paul van Soest, Centre for Energy Conservation and Environmental Technology, Delft, Netherlands, letter to author, 11 October 1995; emissions from Kees Baas, Central Bureau of Statistics, The Hague, e-mail message to author, 3 February 1997.

12. David O'Connor, "The Use of Economic Instruments in Environmental Management: The East Asian Experience," in OECD, *Applying Economic Instruments*, op. cit. note 6.

13. U.S. General Accounting Office (GAO), *Air Pollution: Allowance Trading Offers an Opportunity to Reduce Emissions at Less Cost* (Washington, DC: 1994); industry and government estimates from Martha Hamilton, "Selling Pollution Rights Cuts the Cost of Cleaner Air," *Washington Post*, 24 August 1994; environmentalist estimate and current price from Jessica Mathews, "Environmental Success Story," *Washington Post*, 17 June 1996. Prices expressed per metric ton.

14. Quote from Hamilton, op. cit. note 13; scrubber price decline and savings estimate from GAO, op. cit. note 13.

15. GAO, op. cit. note 13. Environmental taxes can be made analogously revenue-neutral. Governments can tax companies only if they increase pollution above some baseline and subsidize them if they decrease it, an approach that has been called an "incremental tax." See J. Andrew Hoerner and Frank Muller, "The Impact of a Broad-based Energy Tax on the Competitiveness of U.S. Industry," *The Natural Resources Tax Review*, July/August 1993.

16. Mark Sagoff, *The Economy of the Earth: Philosophy, Law, and the Environment* (Cambridge, U.K.: University of Cambridge Press, 1988); Peter Brimblecombe, *The Big Smoke: A History of Pollution in London since Medieval Times* (London: Methuen and Company, 1987); World Resources Institute (WRI), *World Resources 1996–97: A Guide to the Global Environment* (New York: Oxford University Press, 1996).

17. Herman E. Daly and John B. Cobb, Jr., *For the Common Good: Redirecting the Economy toward Community, the Environment, and a Sustainable Future* (Boston: Beacon Press, 1989).

18. Christopher D. Stone, *Earth and Other Ethics: The Case for Moral Pluralism* (New York: Harper & Row, 1987).

19. Tax rates are for chlorofluorocarbon-11, one of the main ozone-depleting chemicals; rates for other chemicals are based on their relative ozone-depletion potential. J. Andrew Hoerner, "Tax Tools for Protecting the Atmosphere: The U.S. Ozone-depleting Chemicals Tax," in Gale and Barg, op. cit. note 1.

20. Sandra Postel, *Last Oasis: Facing Water Scarcity* (New York: W.W. Norton and Company, 1992).

21. Table 1 is based on the following sources: McLeod, op. cit. note 6; Chile from Mateen Thobani, "Tradable Property Rights to Water," FPD Note (Washington, DC: World Bank, Vice Presidency for Finance and Private

Sector Development), February 1995; Germany, Denmark, and Norway from EEA, op. cit. note 5; Netherlands from Bressers and Schuddeboom, op. cit. note 6, and from Baas, op. cit. note 11; Sweden from Ministry of the Environment and Natural Resources (MENR), *The Swedish Experience: Taxes and Charges in Environmental Policy* (Stockholm: 1994); U.S. permit system from GAO, op. cit. note 13; U.S. tax from Hoerner, op. cit. note 19; Singapore from O'Connor, op. cit. note 12; New Jersey from Dana Clark and David Downes, *What Price Biodiversity? Economic Incentives and Biodiversity Conservation in the United States* (Washington, DC: Center for International Environmental Law, 1995), and from John Ross, Pinelands Development Credit Bank, Trenton, discussion with author, 25 March 1997; J. Andrew Hoerner, "The Louisiana Environmental Tax Scorecard," in Gale and Barg, op. cit. note 1. For more complete surveys, see Gale and Barg, op. cit. note 1; OECD, *Applying Economic Instruments*, op. cit. note 6; idem, *Environmental Taxes*, op. cit. note 3; Janet E. Milne, *Environmental Taxes in New England: An Inventory of Environmental Tax and Fee Mechanisms Enacted by New England States and New York* (South Royalton, VT: Environmental Law Center, Vermont Law School, 1996); Victoria P. Summers, "Tax Treatment of Pollution Control in the European and Central Asian Economies in Transition and Other Selected Countries," in Charles E. Walker, Mark A. Bloomfield, and Margot Thorning, eds., *Strategies for Improving Environmental Quality and Increasing Economic Growth* (Washington, DC: Center for Policy Research, in press); and J. Andrew Hoerner, "Life and Taxes," *The Amicus Journal,* summer 1995.

22. Summers, op. cit. note 21; Potier, op. cit. note 6; figure of 1 percent is based on Summers, op. cit. note 21, and on OECD, *Revenue Statistics*, op. cit. note 3.

23. Summers, op. cit. note 21; Potier, op. cit. note 6; "Government to Gradually Implement Program to Tax Polluters, Resource Users," *International Environment Reporter,* 15 October 1996; "NEPA to Impose 'Pollution Tax' on Industry to Curb Dramatic Increase in SO_x Emissions," *International Environment Reporter,* 6 March 1996; "Industry Facing New Tax to Fund Much-needed Water Treatment Projects," *International Environment Reporter,* 15 May 1996.

24. Turkey and Thailand from Earth Summit Watch, Four in '94. *Two Years After Rio: Assessing National Actions to Implement Agenda 21* (New York: Natural Resources Defense Council and Campaign for Action to Protect the Earth, 1994); David Tenenbaum, "The Greening of Costa Rica," *Technology Review,* October 1995.

25. Rögnvaldur Hannesson, "The Political Economy of ITQs," prepared for Symposium on Fisheries Management, University of Washington, Seattle, 14–16 June 1994 (Bergen-Sandviken, Norway: Norwegian School of Economics and Business Administration, 1994); Larry D. Simpson, "Are Water Markets a Viable Option?" *Finance & Development,* June 1994.

26. Revenue totals and shares in this and following paragraph are Worldwatch estimates, using EU figures from EC, op. cit. note 3, and non-EU figures from OECD, *Revenue Statistics,* op. cit. note 3, and from OECD, *Environmental Taxes,* op. cit. note 3. Factors influencing driving from Marcia Lowe, *Shaping Cities: The Environmental and Human Dimensions,* Worldwatch Paper 105 (Washington, DC: Worldwatch Institute, October 1991). Figure 2 is based on T. Sterner, "The Price of Petroleum Products," in Thomas Sterner, ed., *Economic Policies for Sustainable Development* (Dordrecht, Netherlands: Kluwer Academic Publishers, 1994). Gasoline consumption figures from United Nations, *1994 Energy Statistics Yearbook* (New York: 1996). Prices are for premium unleaded, converted to dollars based on purchasing-power parities, and are from OECD, *Energy Prices and Taxes: Third Quarter 1996* (Paris: 1997); however, prices for Denmark, New Zealand, and Japan, where premium unleaded is not sold, are based on those for regular unleaded, adjusted upward by three cents per liter, the average differential in OECD countries that sell both.

27. Belgium and Canada from OECD, *Environmental Taxes,* op. cit. note 3.

28. Australian and Danish ozone-depleter taxes and Danish sand and gravel tax from ibid.; revenue figure is for fiscal years, which begin one quarter before corresponding calendar years, and is from U.S. Office of Management and Budget, *Budget of the United States Government, Fiscal Year 1996,* Historical Tables (Washington, DC: U.S. Government Printing Office, 1997), retrieved via WAIS database search at <http://www.access.gpo.gov/omb/omb003.html>. The U.S. tax was originally intended to absorb windfall profits created by new regulations that restricted the supply of ozone-depleting chemicals, but appears to have been set high enough to have accelerated their phase-out. See Hoerner, op. cit. note 19. Swedish taxes from MENR, op. cit. note 21; Danish waste charge from EEA, op. cit. note 5.

29. Frank Muller, "Mitigating Climate Change: The Case for Energy Taxes," *Environment,* March 1996.

30. California and Massachusetts from David P. Novello, "Capturing the Market's Power," *The Environmental Forum,* September/October 1994; use of fishing permit systems from Rögnvaldur Hannesson, Norwegian School of Economics and Business Administration, Bergen-Sandviken, Norway, discussion with author, 7 June 1995; Alicante from Arthur Maass and Raymond L. Anderson, *...and the Desert Shall Rejoice: Conflict, Growth, and Justice in Arid Environments* (Cambridge, MA: MIT Press, 1978).

31. Postel, op. cit. note 20; Clark and Downes, op. cit. note 21; Ross, op. cit. note 21.

32. Hoerner, "Louisiana Environmental Tax," op. cit. note 21.

33. Carolyn Webber and Aaron Wildavsky, *A History of Taxation and Expenditure in the Western World* (New York: Simon and Schuster, 1986).

34. U.S. figure excludes government subsidies and reduction of property tax base caused by public ownership of land under roads, and is from Charles Komanoff, "Pollution Taxes for Roadway Transportation," *Pace Environmental Law Review*, fall 1994; per-liter estimate is based on fuel usage of 529.9 billion liters for 1993, from U.S. Department of Transportation, Federal Highway Administration, *Highway Statistics 1994* (Washington, DC: 1995), Table MF-21, <http://www.bts.gov/fhwa/yellowbook/section1/mf21.xls>; European studies from EEA, op. cit. note 5; comparisons to tax revenues based on OECD, *Revenue Statistics*, op. cit. note 3. The U.S. payroll tax applies to roughly the first $60,000 in annual wages, so workers earning more would receive a smaller raise in percentage terms.

35. Australia from Department of the Environment, Sport and Territories, *Subsidies to the Use of Natural Resources* (Canberra: 1996); Japan from Jason C. Rylander, "Accounting for Nature: A Look at Attempts to Fashion a 'Green GDP'," *Renewable Resources Journal*, summer 1996; China from Vaclav Smil, "Environmental Change as a Source of Conflict and Economic Loss in China," in Project on Environmental Change and Acute Conflict, Occasional Paper Series, no. 2 (Washington, DC: American Academy of Arts and Sciences, 1992); Hans Diefenbacher, "The Index of Sustainable Economic Welfare: A Case Study of the Federal Republic of Germany," in Clifford W. Cobb and John B. Cobb, Jr., *The Green National Product: A Proposed Index of Sustainable Economic Welfare* (Lanham, MD: University Press of America, 1994); Tim Jackson and Susanna Stymne, *Sustainable Economic Welfare in Sweden: A Pilot Index 1950–1992* (Stockholm: Stockholm Environment Institute, 1996); U.S. from Clifford Cobb, Ted Halstead, and Jonathan Rowe, *The Genuine Progress Indicator: Summary of Data and Methodology* (San Francisco: Redefining Progress, 1995). In the Germany, Sweden, and U.S. studies, damage estimates for loss of wetlands, fertile soil, and old-growth forests, for ozone depletion, and for greenhouse gas buildup reflect current costs of past damage. The appropriate base for environmental taxes would be future costs of current damage, which are of at least comparable magnitude.

36. Current tax levels from OECD, *Revenue Statistics*, op. cit. note 3.

37. Modeling results in this and following paragraph are from John P. Weyant, Stanford University, Energy Modeling Forum, Stanford, CA, draft manuscript, June 1995, and from idem, letter to author, 10 October 1995; carbon content of fuels from Gregg Marland, "Carbon Dioxide Emission Rates for Conventional and Synthetic Fuels," *Energy* 8, no. 12 (1983), and assumes a 90 percent efficiency in converting petroleum to gasoline, based on Thomas B. Johansson et al., "A Renewables-intensive Global Energy Scenario," in Thomas B. Johansson, Birgit Bodlund, and Robert H. Williams, eds., *Renewable Energy: Sources for Fuels and Electricity* (Washington, DC: Island Press, 1993).

38. Concentration stabilization from T.M.L. Wigley, R. Richels, and J.A. Edmonds, "Economic and Environmental Choices in the Stabilization of Atmospheric CO_2 Concentrations," *Nature*, 18 January 1996.

39. Sulfur emissions decline is a Worldwatch estimate, based on WRI, op. cit. note 16; role of regulation from Hilary F. French, *Clearing the Air: A Global Agenda*, Worldwatch Paper 94 (Washington, DC: Worldwatch Institute, January 1990); driving data and emissions standards from Stacy C. Davis and David N. McFarlin, *Transportation Energy Data Book: Edition 16* (Oak Ridge, TN: Oak Ridge National Laboratory (ORNL), 1996), <http://www-cta.ornl.gov/data/tedb16/pdf/tedball.pdf>; emissions data from EPA, Office of Air Quality and Planning Standards, *National Air Pollutant Emission Estimates: 1900–1994* (Research Triangle Park, NC: 1995), Tables A-1, A-2, A-3, <http://www.epa.gov/oar/emtrnd94/trapp_a.pdf>.

40. Robert Repetto, *Jobs, Competitiveness, and Environmental Regulation: What Are the Real Issues?* (Washington, DC: WRI, 1995); Judith M. Dean, "Trade and the Environment: A Survey of the Literature," in Patrick Low, ed., *International Trade and the Environment*, World Bank Discussion Paper 159 (Washington, DC: 1992), quoted in OECD, *Implementation Strategies for Environmental Taxes* (Paris: 1996).

41. Robert Repetto et al., *Has Environmental Protection Really Reduced Productivity Growth? We Need Unbiased Measures* (Washington, DC: WRI, 1996).

42. Michael E. Porter and Claas van der Linde, "Toward a New Conception of the Environment-Competitiveness Relationship," *Journal of Economic Perspectives*, fall 1995.

43. Keith Schneider, "Unbending Regulations Incite Move to Alter Pollution Laws," *New York Times*, 29 November 1993.

44. Michael Renner, *Rethinking the Role of the Automobile*, Worldwatch Paper 84 (Washington, DC: Worldwatch Institute, June 1988).

45. MENR, op. cit. note 21.

46. Gunnar S. Eskeland and Shantayanan Devarajan, *Taxing Bads by Taxing Goods: Pollution Control with Presumptive Charges*, Directions in Development Series (Washington, DC: World Bank, 1996).

47. Steven Nadel and Miriam Pye, *Appliance and Equipment Efficiency Standards: Impacts by State* (Washington, DC, and Berkeley, CA: American Council for an Energy-Efficient Economy, 1996). Savings figures are net of sometimes-higher cost of more efficient appliances.

48. MENR, op. cit. note 21.

49. United States from James Poterba, "Tax Policy to Combat Global Warming: On Designing a Carbon Tax," in Rudiger Dornbusch and James Poterba, eds., *Global Warming: Economic Policy Responses* (Cambridge, MA: MIT Press, 1991; reprint, Cambridge, MA: National Bureau of Economic

Research, 1991); elderly from Economic Opportunity Research Institute, National Council of Senior Citizens (NCSC), and Villers Advocacy Associates (VAA), *Double Jeopardy: The Impact of Energy Taxes on Low-Income Households* (Washington, DC: NCSC and VAA, 1988); developing countries from Christine Kerr and Leslie Citroen, *Household Expenditures on Infrastructure Services*, background paper for *World Development Report 1994* (Washington, DC: World Bank, undated).

50. Portugal from EEA, op. cit. note 5; Netherlands from VROM, op .cit. note 6.

51. Robert Greenstein and Frederick C. Hutchinson, *Offsetting the Effects of Regressive Tax Increases on Low- and Moderate-Income Households* (Washington, DC: Center on Budget and Policy Priorities (CBPP), 1990); Southern Europe from Mark Pearson, "Equity Issues and Carbon Taxes," in OECD, *Climate Change: Designing a Practical Tax System* (Paris: 1993).

52. Nikki Scarancke, Greenpeace, Auckland, and Maori former fisher, discussion with author, 8 October 1995.

53. Hal Bernton, "IFQ Reforms Create Fishing Elite," *Anchorage Daily News*, 6 May 1995; figure of $800 million from Paul Seaton, Alliance Against IFQs, testimony before U.S. Senate, Committee on Commerce, Science, and Transportation, Subcommittee on Oceans and Fisheries, Magnuson Act Field Hearing, Anchorage, AK, 25 March 1995; Timothy Egan, "Fringe Benefits from Oil Give Alaska a Big Payday," *New York Times*, 9 October 1996.

54. Paul Hawken, speech given at First International Conference of CIB TG 16, Tampa, FL, 2 November 1993; coal industry from Christopher Flavin and Nicholas Lenssen, *Power Surge: Guide to the Coming Energy Revolution* (New York: W.W. Norton and Company, 1994).

55. Muller, op. cit. note 29.

56. Hoerner and Muller, op. cit. note 15.

57. Paul Demaret and Raoul Stewardson, "Border Tax Adjustments under GATT and EC Law and General Implications for Environmental Taxes," *Journal of World Trade* 28, no. 4 (1994); Hilary Barnes, "Danish Emissions Tax Gets Go-ahead," Financial Times, 15–16 July 1995; Peter Behr, "Trade Panel Upholds U.S. Auto Fuel Law," *Washington Post*, 1 October 1994; for status of WTO debate, see World Trade Organization, Committee on Trade and the Environment, Report to the WTO Ministerial Conference in Singapore in December (Geneva: 1996), <http://www.wto.org/wto/Trade+Env/envrep.wp5>.

58. Suggestion of international forum from Barbara Bramble, "New Financial Mechanisms for Funding Sustainable Development," in Felix Dodds, ed., *The Way Forward: Beyond Agenda 21* (Washington, DC: Island Press, in press).

59. Flavin and Tunali, op. cit. note 1; Hilary F. French, "Learning from the Ozone Experience," in Lester R. Brown et al., *State of the World 1997* (New York: W.W. Norton and Company, 1997).

60. Flavin and Tunali, op. cit. note 1.

61. Anwar Shah and Bjorn Larsen, *Carbon Taxes, the Greenhouse Effect, and Developing Countries,* background paper for *World Development Report 1992* (Washington, DC: World Bank, 1992); figure of 80 percent is a Worldwatch estimate, based on Joel Darmstadter, Perry D. Teitelbaum, and Jaroslav G. Polach, *Energy in the World Economy: A Statistical Review of Trends in Output, Trade, and Consumption since 1925* (Baltimore, MD: Johns Hopkins University Press for Resources for the Future, 1971), and on G. Marland, R. J. Andres, and T. A. Boden, *Global, Regional, and National CO_2 Emission Estimates from Fossil Fuel Burning, Cement Production, and Gas Flaring: 1950–1994,* revised February 1997 (electronic database) (Oak Ridge, TN: ORNL, 1997), <http://cdiac.esd.ornl.gov/ftp/ndp030r7/emissions-tables/region94.dat>, viewed 3 March 1997; U.N. Development Programme, *Human Development Report 1994* (New York: Oxford University Press, 1994).

62. "New Carbon/Energy Tax Proposal Offered, But United Kingdom Still Seen As Opponent," *International Environment Reporter,* 6 October 1993; "Revised Commission Proposal on CO_2 Calls for Voluntary Taxation Scheme," *International Environment Reporter,* 17 May 1995; "Commission Delays Introduction of Draft Directive on EU-wide Energy Tax," *International Environment Reporter,* 19 February 1997.

63. French, op. cit. note 59; Gary Gardner, "Organic Farming Up Sharply," in Lester R. Brown, Christopher Flavin, and Hal Kane, *Vital Signs 1996: The Trends That Are Shaping Our Future* (New York: W.W. Norton and Company, 1996); Christopher Flavin, "Wind Power Growth Continues," in Lester R. Brown, Michael Renner, and Christopher Flavin, *Vital Signs 1997: The Environmental Trends That Are Shaping Our Future* (New York: W.W. Norton and Company, in press); Molly O'Meara, "Solar Cell Shipments Keep Rising," in Brown, Renner, and Flavin, op. cit. this note; Table 2 is based on EBI, op. cit. note 8.

64. Paul Hawken, "Natural Capitalism," *Mother Jones,* March/April 1997; Herman E. Daly, *Beyond Growth: The Economics of Sustainable Development* (Boston: Beacon Press, 1996).

65. Jodi L. Jacobson, *Gender Bias: Roadblock to Sustainable Development,* Worldwatch Paper 110 (Washington, DC: Worldwatch Institute, September 1992); Hal Kane, "Micro-enterprise," *World Watch,* March/April 1996; Lowe, op. cit. note 26.

66. GDP losses are based on estimates of average "deadweight burden" per dollar of revenue from Dale W. Jorgenson and Yun Kun-Young, *The Excess Burden of Taxation in the U.S.,* Discussion Paper 1528 (Cambridge, MA:

Harvard University, Harvard Institute for Economic Research, 1990), cited in Roger C. Dower and Mary Beth Zimmerman, *The Right Climate for Carbon Taxes: Creating Economic Incentives to Protect the Atmosphere* (Washington, DC: WRI, 1992), and on revenue totals from OECD, *Revenue Statistics,* op. cit. note 3; William Shakespeare, *The Merchant of Venice,* in G. Blakemore Evans, ed., *The Riverside Shakespeare* (Boston: Houghton Mifflin, 1974).

67. Shares of populations paying income tax from Michael P. Todaro, *Economic Development in the Third World,* 2nd ed. (New York: Longman, Inc., 1981); effects of corruption from Shah and Larsen, op. cit. note 61; figures in Table 2 are Worldwatch estimates, based on OECD, *Revenue Statistics,* op. cit. note 3, on World Bank, *World Development Report,* op. cit. note 3, Tables 1 and 12, on idem, *World Development Indicators,* op. cit. note 3, and, *for Russia, on IMF, World Economic Outlook: October 1994* (Washington, DC: 1994), and on Richard Hemming, Adrienne Cheasty, and Ashok K. Lahiri, "The Revenue Decline," in Daniel A. Citrin and Ashok K. Lihiri, eds., *Policy Experiences and Issues in the Baltics, Russia, and Other Countries of the Former Soviet Union,* IMF Occasional Paper 133 (Washington, DC: IMF, 1995).

68. Southern Europe from Anton Steurer, EC, Eurostat, Luxembourg, discussion with author, 30 January 1997.

69. For the argument for a capital gains tax cut, see, for example, American Council for Capital Formation, *Update: Questions and Answers on Capital Gains,* Special Report (Washington, DC: September 1995).

70. Importance of human capital from World Bank, Environment Department, *Expanding the Measure of Wealth: Indicators of Environmentally Sustainable Development* (Washington, DC: in press).

71. Apparent connection between EU unemployment and U.S. wage declines from Rebecca M. Blank, "The Misdiagnosis of Eurosclerosis," *The American Prospect,* January-February 1997; working poor from Kathryn Porter, *Poverty and Income Trends 1995* (Washington, DC: CBPP, in press); EU unemployment figures are for the 15 nations now members, and are from *European Economy,* no. 62 (1996); 1996 figure is a Worldwatch estimate, based on EC, Eurostat, "EU Unemployment: 10.8% in May," press release (Luxembourg: July 1996), <http://europa.eu.int/en/comm/eurostat/press/96-43.pdf>, on EC, Eurostat, "EU Unemployment: 10.9% in October," press release (Luxembourg: December 1996), <http://europa.eu.int/en/comm/eurostat/press/96-80.pdf>, and on EC, Eurostat, "EU Unemployment Falls to 10.8% in December," press release (Luxembourg: February 1997), <http://europa.eu.int/en/comm/eurostat/press/97-13.pdf>.

72. Aaron Bernstein, "Inequality: How the Gap between Rich and Poor Hurts the Economy," *Business Week,* 15 August 1994; Craig R. Whitney, "Europe Isn't Divided in Its Joblessness," *New York Times,* 31 March 1996.

73. "Why Wages Aren't Growing," interview with Gary Burtless, *Challenge*, November-December 1995; Robert Heilbroner, "Ghosts of the ATM Machine," *New Perspectives Quarterly*, spring 1996.

74. Tax increases on lowest quintile from OECD, *The OECD Jobs Study: Taxation, Employment and Unemployment* (Paris: 1995); 1970 figures from Lorenz Jarass and Gustav M. Obermair, "More Jobs, Less Pollution: Tax Incentives and Statutory Levies," *The Natural Resources Tax Review*, November 1994; 1994 figures from Lorenz Jarass, College of Wiesbaden, Wiesbaden, Germany, letters to author, 11 and 27 February 1997. 1970 Germany figure is for the former West Germany only. Unemployment effects from C.R. Bean, P.R.G. Layard, and S.J. Nickell, "The Rise in Unemployment: A Multi-Country Study," *Economica* 53, cited in OECD, op. cit. this note.

75. Effects of lowering wage tax from OECD, op. cit. note 74; unemployment benefits of a progressive wage tax in Europe from ibid..

76. EC, *Growth, Competitiveness, Employment: The Challenges and Ways Forward into the 21st Century*, White Paper (Luxembourg: OOP, 1993); U.S. modeling from Bruce Schillo et al., "The Distributional Impacts of a Carbon Tax," draft report (Washington, DC: EPA, Energy Policy Branch, 4 August 1992). Figure of 1.5 million jobs is a Worldwatch estimate, based on unemployment rates and totals in EC, "EU Unemployment Falls," op. cit. note 71.

77. Lack of modeling of human capital effects from J. Andrew Hoerner, presentation at the Workshop on Ecological Tax Reform, University of Maryland, College Park, 18–19 March 1996.

78. Sweden description from Bohm, op. cit. note 6; Sweden quantity (14.4 billion SKr) from Nordic Council of Ministers, *The Use of Economic Instruments in Nordic Environmental Policy* (Copenhagen: 1996), cited in Stefan Speck, Keele University, Department of Economics, Keele, Staffordshire, U.K., e-mail message to author, 11 February 1997; Denmark 1994 description and quantity (12 billion DKr) from Andersen, op. cit. note 6; Netherlands description from VROM, op. cit. note 6; Netherlands quantity (2.2 billion Dfl) from Koos van der Vaart, Ministry of Finance, The Hague, discussion with author, 18 December 1995; Spain description from Schröder, op. cit. note 6; Spain quantity (47.47 billion Pta) from Jaun-José Escobar, Ministry of Economy and Finance, Madrid, letter to author, 29 January 1997; Denmark 1996 description and quantity (2.675 billion DKr) from Ministry of Finance, *Energy Tax on Industry* (Oslo: 1995); United Kingdom description and quantity (£450 million) from "Landfill Tax Regime Takes Shape," op. cit. note 6; total tax revenues for all countries from OECD, *Revenue Statistics*, op. cit. note 3.

79. Dawn Erlandson, "The Btu Tax Experience: What Happened and Why It Happened," *Pace Environmental Law Review*, fall 1994; idem, Friends of the Earth, Washington, DC, discussion with author, 11 May 1995.

80. Charles Victor Barber, Nels C. Johnson, and Emmy Hafild, *Breaking the Logjam: Obstacles to Forest Policy Reform in Indonesia and the United States* (Washington, DC: WRI, 1994); Seaton, op. cit. note 53; Egan, op. cit. note 53.

81. Western Europe from Thomas Sterner, Gothenburg University, Department of Economics, Gothenburg, Sweden, discussion with author, 6 February 1996; Bressers and Schuddeboom, op. cit. note 6.

82. Andersen, op. cit. note 9; underfunding of environmental agencies in developing countries from Potier, op. cit. note 6, and from Sergio Margulis, "The Use of Economic Instruments in Environmental Policies: The Experiences of Brazil, Mexico, Chile and Argentina," in OECD, *Applying Economic Instruments,* op. cit. note 6.

83. François Bregha and John Moffet, "The Tax for Fuel Conservation in Ontario," in Gale and Barg, op. cit. note 1; strengths of feebates from Daniel Lashof, "Cool Solutions for Global Warming," *Technology Review,* February/March 1996.

84. Roodman, op. cit. note 3.

85. Stefan Bach, Michael Kohlhaas, and Barbara Praetorius, "Ecological Tax Reform Even If Germany Has to Go It Alone," *Economic Bulletin* (Berlin: German Institute for Economic Research (DIW)), July 1994.

86. Worldwatch estimates, based on Statistisches Bundesamt, *Volkswirtschaftliche Gesamtrechnungen* (Stuttgart: Metzler-Poeschel, 1990), on Michael Kohlhaas, DIW, Berlin, letter to author, 20 June 1995, and on Hans Wessels, DIW, Berlin, letter to author, 10 August 1995.

87. Kristina Steenbock, consultant to Greenpeace Germany, New York, discussion with author, 16 June 1995; "Group Gets Support for CO_2 Tax from 16 German Producers, Service Industries," *International Environment Reporter,* 21 September 1994; "Big 3 Carmakers Back Higher Gasoline Taxes," *Journal of Commerce,* 21 December 1992; "Eco-tax Possibility Dwindling in Face of Industry Opposition, Unemployment," *International Environment Reporter,* 1 May 1996.

88. Stewart, op. cit. note 5; EEA, op. cit. note 5.

89. Hoerner, op. cit. note 77; Jeffrey H. Birnbaum and Alan S. Murray, *Showdown at Gucci Gulch: Lawmakers, Lobbyists, and the Unlikely Triumph of Tax Reform* (New York: Vintage Books, 1987).

PUBLICATION ORDER FORM

_____ *State of the World:* $13.95
The annual book used by journalists, activists, scholars, and policymakers worldwide to get a clear picture of the environmental problems we face.

_____ *Vital Signs:* $12.00
The book of trends that are shaping our future in easy to read graph and table format, with a brief commentary on each trend.

_____ **Subscription to WORLD WATCH magazine: $20.00 (international airmail $35.00)**
Stay abreast of global environmental trends and issues with our award-winning, eminently readable bimonthly magazine.

_____ **Worldwatch Library: $30.00 (international subscribers $45.00)**
Receive *State of the World* and all six Worldwatch Papers as they are released during the calendar year.

_____ **Worldwatch Database Disk Subscription: $89.00**
Contains global agricultural, energy, economic, environmental, social, and military indicators from all current Worldwatch publications including this Paper. Includes a mid-year update, and *Vital Signs* and *State of the World* as they are published. Can be used with Lotus 1-2-3, Quattro Pro, Excel, SuperCalc and many other spreadsheets. **Check one:** _____ **IBM-compatible or** _____ **Macintosh**

_____ **Worldwatch Papers—See complete list on following page**
Single copy: $5.00 • 2–5: $4.00 ea. • 6–20: $3.00 ea. • 21 or more: $2.00 ea. Call Director of Communication, at (202) 452-1999, for discounts on larger orders.

$4.00 Shipping and Handling *($8.00 outside North America)*

_____ **TOTAL**

Make check payable to Worldwatch Institute
1776 Massachusetts Ave., NW, Washington, DC 20036-1904 USA

Enclosed is my check or purchase order for U.S. $_____

☐ AMEX ☐ VISA ☐ MasterCard _____
                                          Card Number   Expiration Date

_____
name   **daytime phone #**

_____
address

_____
city   **state**   **zip/country**

**phone: (202) 452-1999   fax: (202) 296-7365   e-mail: wwpub@worldwatch.org
website: www.worldwatch.org**

☐ **Send me a brochure of all Worldwatch publications.**

Worldwatch Papers

No. of Copies

_____ 90. **The Bicycle: Vehicle for a Small Planet** by Marcia D. Lowe
_____ 92. **Poverty and the Environment: Reversing the Downward Spiral** by Alan B. Durning
•_____ 94. **Clearing the Air: A Global Agenda** by Hilary F. French
_____ 95. **Apartheid's Environmental Toll** by Alan B. Durning
_____ 96. **Swords Into Plowshares: Converting to a Peace Economy** by Michael Renner
_____ 97. **The Global Politics of Abortion** by Jodi L. Jacobson
_____ 98. **Alternatives to the Automobile: Transport for Livable Cities** by Marcia D. Lowe
_____100. **Beyond the Petroleum Age: Designing a Solar Economy** by Christopher Flavin
          and Nicholas Lenssen
_____101. **Discarding the Throwaway Society** by John E. Young
_____102. **Women's Reproductive Health: The Silent Emergency** by Jodi L. Jacobson
_____104. **Jobs in a Sustainable Economy** by Michael Renner
_____105. **Shaping Cities: The Environmental and Human Dimensions** by Marcia D. Lowe
_____106. **Nuclear Waste: The Problem That Won't Go Away** by Nicholas Lenssen
_____107. **After the Earth Summit: The Future of Environmental Governance**
          by Hilary F. French
_____109. **Mining the Earth** by John E. Young
_____110. **Gender Bias: Roadblock to Sustainable Development** by Jodi L. Jacobson
_____111. **Empowering Development: The New Energy Equation** by Nicholas Lenssen
_____112. **Guardians of the Land: Indigenous Peoples and the Health of the Earth**
          by Alan Thein Durning
_____113. **Costly Tradeoffs: Reconciling Trade and the Environment** by Hilary F. French
_____114. **Critical Juncture: The Future of Peacekeeping** by Michael Renner
_____115. **Global Network: Computers in a Sustainable Society** by John E. Young
_____116. **Abandoned Seas: Reversing the Decline of the Oceans** by Peter Weber
_____117. **Saving the Forests: What Will It Take?** by Alan Thein Durning
_____118. **Back on Track: The Global Rail Revival** by Marcia D. Lowe
_____119. **Powering the Future: Blueprint for a Sustainable Electricity Industry**
          by Christopher Flavin and Nicholas Lenssen
_____120. **Net Loss: Fish, Jobs, and the Marine Environment** by Peter Weber
_____121. **The Next Efficiency Revolution: Creating a Sustainable Materials Economy**
          by John E. Young and Aaron Sachs
_____122. **Budgeting for Disarmament: The Costs of War and Peace** by Michael Renner
_____123. **High Priorities: Conserving Mountain Ecosystems and Cultures**
          by Derek Denniston
_____124. **A Building Revolution: How Ecology and Health Concerns Are Transforming
          Construction** by David Malin Roodman and Nicholas Lenssen
_____125. **The Hour of Departure: Forces That Create Refugees and Migrants** by Hal Kane.
_____126. **Partnership for the Planet: An Environmental Agenda for the United Nations**
          by Hilary F. French
———127. **Eco-Justice: Linking Human Rights and the Environment** by Aaron Sachs
_____128. **Imperiled Waters, Impoverished Future: The Decline of Freshwater Ecosystems**
          by Janet N. Abramovitz
_____129. **Infecting Ourselves: How Environmental and Social Disruptions Trigger Disease**
          by Anne E. Platt
_____130. **Climate of Hope: New Strategies for Stabilizing the World's Atmosphere**
          by Christopher Flavin and Odil Tunali
_____131. **Shrinking Fields: Cropland Loss in a World of Eight Billion** by Gary Gardner
_____132. **Dividing the Waters: Food Security, Ecosystem Health, and the New Politics of
          Scarcity** by Sandra Postel
_____133. **Paying the Piper: Subsidies, Politics, and the Environment** by David Malin Roodman
_____134. **Getting the Signals Right: Tax Reform to Protect the Environment and the Economy**
          by David Malin Roodman

_____ **Total copies (transfer number to order form on previous page)**